Europe and Global Security

Edited by Bastian Giegerich

Europe and Global Security

Edited by Bastian Giegerich

IISS The International Institute for Strategic Studies

The International Institute for Strategic Studies

Arundel House | 13–15 Arundel Street | Temple Place | London | WC2R 3DX | UK

First published November 2010 by **Routledge**
4 Park Square, Milton Park, Abingdon, Oxon, OX14 4RN

for **The International Institute for Strategic Studies**
Arundel House, 13–15 Arundel Street, Temple Place, London, WC2R 3DX, UK
www.iiss.org

Simultaneously published in the USA and Canada by **Routledge**
270 Madison Ave., New York, NY 10016

Routledge is an imprint of Taylor & Francis, an Informa Business

© 2010 The International Institute for Strategic Studies

DIRECTOR-GENERAL AND CHIEF EXECUTIVE John Chipman
EDITOR Tim Huxley
MANAGER FOR EDITORIAL SERVICES Ayse Abdullah
ASSISTANT EDITOR Janis Lee
COVER/PRODUCTION John Buck

The International Institute for Strategic Studies is an independent centre for research, information and debate on the problems of conflict, however caused, that have, or potentially have, an important military content. The Council and Staff of the Institute are international and its membership is drawn from almost 100 countries. The Institute is independent and it alone decides what activities to conduct. It owes no allegiance to any government, any group of governments or any political or other organisation. The IISS stresses rigorous research with a forward-looking policy orientation and places particular emphasis on bringing new perspectives to the strategic debate.

The Institute's publications are designed to meet the needs of a wider audience than its own membership and are available on subscription, by mail order and in good bookshops. Further details at www.iiss.org.

Printed and bound in Great Britain by Bell & Bain Ltd, Thornliebank, Glasgow

British Library Cataloguing in Publication Data
A catalogue record for this book is available from the British Library

Library of Congress Cataloging in Publication Data

ADELPHI series
ISSN 0567-932X

ADELPHI 414–415
ISBN 978-0-415-66934-4

Contents

ACKNOWLEDGEMENTS

This book arose out of a two-year research project the IISS conducted in 2008 and 2009 with the generous support of the European Commission under the Seventh Framework Programme. The project (FORESEC) analysed trends and drivers in Europe's evolving security situation and provided a framework for different members of the IISS research programme to bring their combined expertise to bear on a set of common questions. Some of the chapters were first drafted in the FORESEC project, whereas others were written specifically for this book.

INTRODUCTION

Bastian Giegerich

Despite the European Union's struggles to combine the different aspects of security policy into a coherent whole, a discourse has emerged suggesting that as a security actor it might be uniquely placed to address security challenges of the present and the future. The key arguments to support such a view are that, insofar as it can draw on community and member states' capacity, the EU can potentially command an impressive array of instruments, ranging from the political and societal to the economic and military. In other words, the EU is assumed to be a comprehensive actor. As the former EU commissioner for external relations, Benita Ferrero-Waldner, explained, by combining hard and soft power instruments the EU aspired to 'smart power' status[1]. Secondly, scholars such as Martin Ortega, then a researcher at the EU's Institute for Security Studies, suggest the EU enjoys great international political legitimacy because it is driven by a benign, rule-bound multilateralism:

> The EU is *not* attempting to compete militarily with other world powers, the EU is *not* building up a military capacity independent of that of its member states,

> the EU is *not* trying to acquire WMD, the EU has *no*
> territorial claims to make, the EU does *not* intend to
> intervene militarily to change regimes, and the EU is
> determined to work hand-in-hand with the United
> Nations. In short as it embodies a new category of
> international actor, the EU's approach to global rela-
> tions is different from the traditional approach of
> major powers. As a consequence, the rest of the world
> welcomes the European Union as a new kind of more
> constructive actor in global relations.[2]

Its distinctive composition and status led to the conclusion that
the EU might be a promising framework for member states to
conduct security policy in a context of global power shifts and
increasing complexity, where security challenges can no longer
be pressed into categories such as 'internal' or 'external' and
'civilian' or 'military'.

In light of such optimistic and far-reaching assumptions, it
should not come as a surprise that external observers sometimes offer scathing critiques of European security debates, as
exemplified by historian Robert Kagan's infamous assessment
that Europeans only de-emphasise military instruments in their
security policy because they have so few of them, and that they
tend not to perceive threats to be pressing because European
military shortfalls leave them unable to act on problems.[3] It is the
'psychology of the weak' that makes Europe look for purpose in
comprehensiveness and legitimacy, says Kagan. In the extreme
this argument is certainly unconvincing. Leaving aside the
potentially circular argument about the utility of military force
and the alleged weakness of European capabilities, there is no
reason why only military great powers should be able to accurately perceive threats and it is by no means clear that they would
come to similar conclusions as to how to respond to threats.

The EU Security Strategy, first written in 2003 and reviewed in 2008, codifies several underlying principles.[4] It establishes that European security policy should be holistic in the sense of bringing together policy instruments, that it should be multi-lateral and aimed at the prevention of security risk – and hence that it should be concerned with the root causes of threats. Thus, security challenges are defined in terms of a threat assessment, whereby large-scale aggression against EU member states is judged to be unlikely, and international terrorism, the prolifer-ation of weapons of mass destruction, regional conflicts, failed states and organised crime present the core worries. These key threats, as the EU argues, have to be seen in the context of drivers and multipliers, such as poverty, climate change, resource scarcity and migration.

Much of the thinking behind the European Security Strategy is expressed in the security and defence reviews conducted in major member states. For example, the 2008 French White Paper on national defence and security argues:

> the security of France, similarly to that of Europe, must ... be understood in a global way. The national security strategy encompasses both external and inter-nal security, military as well as civilian, economic and diplomatic means. It has to consider all phenomena, risks and threats potentially detrimental to the way of life of the nation.[5]

Similarly, the United Kingdom's 2009 security strategy insists new challenges 'have transformed our way of understanding national security, away from the traditional focus of threats to the state and its interests from other states. These are still important. But ... the focus has shifted to a diverse but interconnected set of threats and risks to the UK and our citizens, both directly and through wider international instability.'[6] The coalition government of Conservatives and Liberal Democrats, formed after the May 2010 general election, echoed this sentiment, arguing in their October 2010 security strategy that 'the risk picture is likely to become increasingly diverse. No single risk will dominate ... Therefore, achieving security will become more complex.'[7]

Countries and institutions alike now share a common security space. Rigid, box-like divisions between civil and military security and internal and external security are no longer realistic, since contemporary security threats are seldom confined within geographical and institutional boundaries. Thus, in the past 20 years European security has undeniably become more complex. New security threats and risks have emerged, posed by non-traditional actors, and security advisers and defence ministers are now paying heed to a number of issues which, up until a few years ago, would not have been considered security threats. Such profound changes clearly raise the question of who should be tasked with the responsibility for providing security.

The EU's concept of security is unsurprisingly not driven by the nation state as the referent object of security. Sovereignty has been subjected to re-examination as member states move towards greater integration. In its updated form, attenuated by and shared among member governments, the concept is yet to be formally adopted at the EU level. The process of European integration as such has historically been driven by the attempt to contain and balance the competing interests of sovereign states; the fact that integration began in the first half of the twentieth century in the sectors of coal and steel – with their obvious links to armaments production – underlines this point. More recently, EU leaders point to the reality that 'no EU-member state is a global player any more. There is no future for vanity in a country alone.'[8]

By and large the EU is bound by and seeks to promote a rule-based system to govern international behaviour. In its dealings with other international actors it prioritises good governance; social, economic and political reform; trade and uninterrupted access to markets; and respect for human rights and the rule of law. In essence, the EU is seeking to remake international relations in its own image. The logic of this approach is rooted in the belief that exporting the EU model will make the world safer by bringing prosperity, freedom and social stability. Herman van Rompuy, who in 2009 was appointed the president of the European Council – the body through which EU member-state governments define priorities and provide direction for the Union – said in 2010: 'I am convinced that the world will move in the direction of the European model, sooner or later.'[9] While van Rompuy was not speaking about security policy, but rather about the EU's social, economic and political dimensions, his words echo the belief among European leaders that the Union's founding values will attract an international following. At the same time, Europe realises it 'can no longer rely on [its] ability to set the world agenda, and the need to build alliances and consensus with the newly emerging powers will only continue to grow'.[10] The salience of the EU as a security actor thus hinges on its supposed comprehensiveness and its ability to be recognised as a legitimate international actor. Hence, it is worthwhile to briefly contemplate the consequences of the shifting international system.

Globally, power will be dispersed more widely and the number of power centres is set to increase. The changing structure of the international system and the distribution of power potential will result in relative decline: the EU and its member states will definitely lose some influence in world affairs, at least measured in traditional terms such as economics and demographics. In demographic terms, world population is

projected to rise to more than 9 billion by 2050. The EU's population, based on current member states, is set to decline to less
than 5.4% of world population from its current 7.2%. India will
overtake China as the most populous country by 2030 and by
2050 is expected to have a population of some 1.6bn, or 17.6%
of world population (roughly equalling its share today). EU
member states will continue to have the oldest population of
all major actors, with a median age of 47 in 2050 (unchanged
from 2030). The worldwide median age is expected to rise to 34
by 2030 and 38 by 2050. Much of the global growth will occur
outside of the countries commonly understood to be candidates for great-power status. The most worrying statistic in
terms of the current demographic situation is that the population in EU member states has a (weighted) median age of 41
years, compared to a worldwide median age of 29.[11]

In economic terms the changes can be expected to be even
more dramatic. Year-on-year per capita growth rates in the
BRIC countries (Brazil, Russia, India and China) are expected
to be three to four times higher than those in the US and EU
member states, which does spell a relative economic decline for
the latter. In terms of the overall size of the economies, China is
expected to be the world's largest by 2050. It should be noted,
however, that wealth will continue to be distributed unevenly.
Even though BRIC economies are expected to grow very quickly,
they are not expected to catch up with EU member-state economies or the US in terms of per capita GDP. In economic terms,
the future dominance of China and India should not be over-
stated: despite a comparatively much smaller share of world
population, the US and EU economies combined accounted for
approximately 54% of world GDP in 2008.[12]

While the international system seems to be in a state of fluid-
ity that defies neat labels such as 'unipolarity' or 'multipolarity',
there is consensus among observers that on most measures of

power the global centre of gravity is shifting towards Asia. The impact of the structure and power redistribution in the international system is likely to be mediated through what can best be described as the nature of relations among major powers. If, as the result of the rise of several countries to great-power status, the role of multilateral institutions and global governance structures diminishes and at the same time great-power rivalries increase, EU member states can be expected to see their loss of influence magnified. This is because the guiding principles of EU foreign and security policy are based on effective multilateralism and cooperation rather than confrontation, and on rule-based interaction rather than the aggressive assertion of military and economic power.

A side effect of power becoming more dispersed among actors with different views of the world, the international system, and key concepts such as sovereignty and multilateralism, is that those different attitudes will become more important. Political scientist Ivan Krastev has argued that there exists a 'fundamental political incompatibility' between Russia and the EU, pitting the postmodern entity that is the EU against more traditional concepts of the state in Russia.[13] Whereas for EU member states concepts such as autonomy and sovereignty have been altered through EU membership, the same is not true for other major international players who often promote traditional notions of these terms centred on the nation-state and its limited permeability as far as international law is concerned.

It is unclear whether the emerging system will be conflict ridden, because economic interdependencies and the growth of international institutions can be expected to have a constraining effect on great-power rivalries.[14] Giovanni Grevi, now a senior researcher at the Madrid-based think tank FRIDE, has argued that 'the challenge lies in finding a new match between power and governance'.[15] He has suggested that the world might witness the emergence of an interpolar system, in which interest-based cooperation among major interdependent power centres has to be channelled through processes of multilateral cooperation. The return of great-power politics is nonetheless a possibility and one that the EU might find difficult to deal with given that its conception of the international system and its self-perception are driven by effective multilateralism.[16]

In 2007 a global opinion poll asked some 57,000 people from more than 50 countries whether the world would benefit from an increase or decrease of the influence of major powers. According to the findings, the EU is the most popular power centre, lending some support to the hypothesis that depicts the EU as commanding considerable soft power.[17] This result is somewhat contradicted by a study that looked into the level of support EU member states receive from other governments for human-rights positions they take in the UN general assembly. Support is here measured as the frequency with which other states have voted with the EU, China, Russia and the US expressed as a percentage. The study found that the level of support for positions the EU members adopted dropped from 72% during the 1997/98 General Assembly session to 55% in the 2007/08 session.[18] While EU internal cohesion on these matters is high, the changing international context apparently creates a legitimacy crisis for the EU, meaning that it is finding it more difficult to organise support for its positions within the UN. What emerges from these polls is thus a stark difference between the EU's ability to sway global public opinion and its ability to effectively engage governments from across the world.

This volume combines the expertise of different parts of the IISS research programme to look at how important security challenges manifest themselves for the EU and to what degree the EU is able to deal with them. Abstract debates about the nature of the EU's security presence and theoretical explanations for shortfalls and advances have been dealt with elsewhere. For our purposes, discussion will focus on the particular set of security challenges facing the EU and its ability to make a contribution in those areas, including the EU's capabilities for civilian and military crisis-management operations and the EU's relations with major powers around the globe, as well as security policy itself as it relates to demographics and migration, terrorism, the proliferation of WMD, energy, climate change and extreme environmental events, and critical infrastructure protection. The body of work suggests that one can indeed witness the beginnings of a specific EU way of doing security policy.[19] This book will help to understand its potential and limitations.

CHAPTER ONE

The European Union and the Major Powers

François Heisbourg
Chairman, International Institute for Strategic Studies

The European Union is not a state: this negative categorisation, which must be the essential starting point of any analysis of EU foreign and security policy, applies most vividly to relations with the major powers, whether these are of a unitary or, as is more frequently the case, a federal nature. Whereas territorial, demographic and economic indicators clearly put the EU in the 'major power' category, the production of foreign, security and defence policy remains rooted in the member states. Nevertheless, the EU has a very real presence in terms of its relations with major powers which needs to be characterised.

What is the EU?
In describing the EU, expressions such as a 'hybrid 'or *sui generis* power are readily used.[1] The Union has become a prime mover in producing laws and regulations governing the domestic life of the populations living within its confines. The extraordinary scope and depth of the *acquis communautaire* become apparent whenever membership negotiations are conducted with new candidate countries. Although one has to treat with caution statistics stating that more than half of the laws and regulations

applying within the EU are the product of Union institutions, the fact is that over the decades, the process of European integration has grown from narrow issues (the Coal and Steel Community of the early 1950s, which established a common market for those commodities among Belgium, France, Italy, Luxembourg, the Netherlands and West Germany) to cover a broad range of competences. In many areas, the EU is as or more federal than some of the major powers: take, for instance, EU rules governing the protection of threatened species, the trade definition of chocolate, the free movement of workers, or the European arrest warrant. However, for contemporary major powers such as Brazil, China, India, Russia and the US, diplomacy, security and defence are in the hands of central government. This 'upside-down' nature of EU competences compared to those of other major (and minor) players is an important shaping – and complicating – factor of the Union's relations with the great powers.

From this characteristic flows another description of the EU as a 'normative empire'.[2] Because its institutions and processes cover such a broad range of activities, and because its geographic sphere of influence puts it in the world league as a market and a partner more generally (see Tables 1–2), the European Union also presents itself as a shaper of global rules and standards. A Chinese toy factory or a cocoa plantation in Côte d'Ivoire will ignore at their peril the existence of European norms and definitions. Major American firms merging will duly file their applications to the European Commission, in much the same way that similar EU-based firms will not complete a merger before going to the relevant US authorities. Beyond the raw weight of vital statistics, the EU appears as one of a club of two global players when it comes to such normative power. One may be tempted to add that the EU's standard-setting power extends beyond the realm of broadly defined market relations

Table 1: **Power Rankings**

Estimated Population in millions for 2010	
China	1,354
India	1,214
European Union*	501
USA	317
Indonesia	232
Brazil	195
Pakistan	184
Bangladesh	164
Nigeria	158
Russia	140
Japan	127
Mexico	108

Source: Population Division of the Department of Economic and Social Affairs of the United Nations Secretariat, *World Population Prospects: The 2008 Revision*, http://esa.un.org/unpp
* Statistic for EU27 from Eurostat

Table 2: **2009 Gross Domestic Product ($bn) PPP(*)**

European Union	*14,739*
USA	14,256
China	8,765
Japan	4,159
India	3,526
Germany	2,806
UK	2,139
Russia	2,109
France	2,108
Brazil	2,013

(*) in excess of $2,000 bn. Source: IMF, World Economic Outlook Database, estimates for 2009

to the production of global values (such as international criminal justice) and goals (cutting carbon emissions). However, the 'normative empire' suffers from two basic problems. The first is the EU's inability and reluctance to back up its production of standards with the hard-power tools that may be necessary to ensure its basic security.[3] The other is linked to its limited ability to turn its norm-setting potential into a 'bankable' commodity in terms of power relations with the major players. Norm-setting has been eminently bankable in other aspects of the EU's business, in terms of membership negotiations or neighbourhood policy. But when it comes to relations with India,

Brazil or the US, the picture is rather less straightforward. The difficulties it has in using its considerable norm-setting power to shape its overall relationship with a Russia that is economically and demographically weaker than the EU bear testimony to a basic problem: norm-setting is to a major extent a molecular, bottom-up and organic process, which doesn't make it easy to use as a currency of power. The existence of a common position defended by the relevant EU bodies will not readily translate into the kind of throw-weight which single-minded major powers can wield, even when the latter have little to bring to the table. The December 2009 climate change summit in Copenhagen was an object lesson in this regard, with China and the US playing a pivotal role while even a united Europe with a strong substantive position was sidelined.

Although the EU is not a state, it has some elements of state power, with certain areas being run along similar lines to their counterparts in major powers. Whereas 'normal' states are unlimited liability partnerships within their borders, the EU is a limited liability partnership, in which competencies in fields such as external trade, foreign aid or competition policy are practically indistinguishable from their US equivalents: the EU commissioner for external trade and the US special trade representative are nearly identical. The same remark could be made concerning the head of the European Central Bank and the chairman of the US Federal Reserve. In such specific cases, there is no functional asymmetry between the EU and the major powers: the head of the Chinese central bank, the chief of the United States Agency for International Development or the Brazilian foreign trade supremo knows exactly which telephone number to dial if he wants to speak to 'Europe'. However, this does not mean the EU can be considered as a proto-state, an *Etat en puissance*: these sectoral competencies are not bound together by the political equivalent of connective tissue. A liver, a heart and a brain operating on side-by-side life support do not constitute a human body. In this respect, the EU resists comparison to Thomas Hobbes's Leviathan. It possesses neither a body nor a personality in the way that Hobbes envisaged seventeenth-century nation-states. Nation-states may be incoherent and inconsistent, but they possess a singleness of political identity and authority which the EU does not.

Nonetheless, the EU as an actor has an existence going well beyond the areas of autonomous power already mentioned. The EU can and does formulate common positions on major foreign and security policy, and has been doing so well before the establishment of a Common Foreign and Security Policy. For instance, ground-breaking language on the Israeli–Palestinian conflict was formulated by the EU's forerunner, the European Economic Community, in May 1980 in the prescient Venice Declaration, which acknowledged the legitimate rights of the Palestinian people and the right of the Palestinian Liberation Organisation to be a part of the peace process.[4] It is no doubt easy to point out the lack of effective follow-through: the same can be said of the limited success of the major powers in dealing with the same set of issues. Furthermore, the EU has been broad-gauged in its foreign and security policy, playing a notable role from Aceh and Timor Leste to Darfur and the Democratic Republic of the Congo. Here again, the limits can be easily pointed out: it is easier to speak and act as one in Timor Leste than it is to have an EU strategy with regard to China. The ability or indeed inability of the EU to exert influence is the direct result of agreement among its members, and notably of those that are the most able and willing to wield state power, on the basis of a common or at least convergent set of decisions. European Political Cooperation and subsequently Common Foreign and Security Policy (CFSP) and Common Security and Defence Policy (CSDP) have an intergovernmental DNA. For the major powers, this means that more effort will be put into dealing with the national fountainheads of EU policy (France, the UK and Germany on Iran; Poland and Germany on Ukraine etc.) than with downstream activity in Brussels.

It would be wrong, however, to equate this mode of operation to a traditional intergovernmental organisation, whether regional, such as NATO or the Organisation for Security and Cooperation in Europe, or global, such as the UN system: the breadth and depth of competencies of the EU makes such a comparison invalid. It bears a resemblance to the Holy Roman Empire, in which the views of the grand electors were essential to the emergence (and over time, disappearance) of a collective will.[5] Overall, the EU appears as an extraordinarily complex and confusing composite of disparate characteristics: a non-state; a normative empire without hard power; a more-or-less disjointed set of issue-specific quasi-state power centres; a latter-day equivalent of the Holy Roman Empire. From the standpoint of the major powers, this mix of characteristics can easily lead to miscalculation, all the more readily fuelled by the difficulties the Europeans themselves have in defining the existential goals, the political nature and territorial extent of their Union. Often the kind of language emanating from Brussels about EU security strategies increases the possibility for misunderstanding, given the disconnect between broad ambitions and limited means.[6] Europe's self-presentation as a power with a strategy also invites scrutiny about its hard-power.

The major powers: the US, China, Russia, Japan, India and Brazil

Major powers are considered to be all of those non-EU countries which figure in all three of the top-ten rankings of the most basic criteria of power (population, GDP and defence spending), and which exceed certain thresholds in absolute value (more than 100 million inhabitants, a GDP exceeding $2 trillion and defence spending of at least $30 billion). It is worth noting that the table is in a state of flux. The 100m population threshold will be breached before 2030 by Vietnam, the Philippines and Egypt, and possibly others. Mexico, South Korea and Turkey are approaching the GDP threshold: multipolarity is becoming a descriptive norm rather than a political eventuality. The recent growth of the Chinese, Indian and Brazilian military budgets has been spectacular, with South Korea poised to reach the $30bn threshold.

In effect, the European Union and its predecessors have been through several stages in terms of relations with major powers, beginning with the first decades of the Cold War, in which the nascent European institutions operated in a purely bipolar world dominated by a friendly US and a threatening Soviet Union. In the latter part of the Cold War a putative triad of democratic power-centres emerged, with the rise of Europe and Japan, while the US clearly remained in a class of its own, given the 'currency of power' prevailing at the time, with ideological drive and strategic reach counting above all in the contest with the Soviet bloc. After this came the brief 'unipolar moment' of the 1990s, during which the US stood alone as a superpower following the collapse of the USSR, while none of the emerging countries had acquired the economic weight or the military reach of any of the major European countries.[7] Finally, the 'multipolar eruption' from the turn of the twenty-first century saw several countries approach (for example, India and Brazil) or exceed (China) the economic power and military spending of any single EU member state. This process will continue to play out, in quantitative terms, with other emerging powers (Indonesia, Turkey) eventually joining the list, and from a qualitative standpoint, as the gap narrows between the US and China. The parallel rise of the non-European powers and the erosion of US primacy will be the backdrop against which the European Union's relations with the major powers will play out.

America first

The EU relationship possesses the stability – and indeed the inertia – which comes from more than 60 years of Euro-Atlantic intimacy involving a deeply held set of similar if not identical values, and shared interests in the strategic and economic arenas. Whatever its limitations, the Atlantic Alliance remains without parallel in the world. Historically, European integration and the Atlantic Alliance were companion projects, made possible by the American decision to station forces and enter into a binding defence commitment in Europe. Because it was both lopsided and intimate, this relationship has rarely been comfortable and has occasionally been fraught, but it has proven to be extraordinarily resilient. The numerous shocks or challenges to the original American–European compact have not led to a basic transformation, let alone disappearance, of the fundamental traits that characterised relations in the aftermath of the Second World War. Thus, a mutual defence obligation, in which the Europeans have never ceased to be the weaker party, continues to exist alongside the individual bilateral ties. For all EU members, the bilateral relationship with the US is broader gauged and deeper rooted, in good times as in bad, than any other relationship with other non-EU members.

This situation is without prejudice to the future role of *NATO*-qua-*NATO*: important as the organisation may be, notably for some of its smaller European members for whom it represents a partial substitute for a national defence policy and effort, NATO is only one tool among many from the US perspective, and a much less important one than it was during the Cold War and the subsequent wars of Yugoslav succession.

Conversely, NATO provides the EU and its members a multi-lateral forum and decision-making body and occasionally an alternative to the bilateral 'hub and spokes' leadership of the US. In this respect, the EU needs to continue to invest in the establishment of a solid CSDP–NATO interface.

The overriding importance and durable intimacy of the US–European relationship poses a peculiar challenge to the EU. There is little if any prospect for transformation into a *'Directoire'* between two equal and similar parties, of the kind originally proposed by Charles de Gaulle in 1958. Euro-Atlantic habits are deeply engrained, because the EU is not a state and because change is fractious (it took more than ten years for the US to move from open hostility to overt accep-tance of a unified European security policy) and of limited significance – at the end of the day, the transatlantic security relationship has hardly changed as a result of the CSDP.[8] This was true in the past when Europe was economically dynamic but strategically dependent in a bipolar world, and it applies no less at a time of European economic and military weak-ness in a multipolar world. The erosion of US primacy, the absence of major strategic threats in the European space and the decline of Europe's strategic role as the emerging powers acquire military reach and political heft will not necessarily cause the estrangement of the Euro-Atlantic allies. Indeed, the contrary probably applies: as the dangers in the Middle Eastern neighbourhood multiply and emerging powers invest in their military might, a soft-power EU has cause to continue to prize the alliance with the US.[9] At the same time, the chances of substantially re-inventing the relationship are limited by the legacies of the past and by the nature of the EU. On the other hand, disagreement on how to deal with an assertive and powerful China or a nuclear Iran could break the transatlantic community. The crisis in the EU, NATO and the UN following the Iraq invasion of 2003 was in this sense a warning of what could lie in store.

Rising China

The unsatisfactory state of EU–China relations has been described in a 2009 publication of the European Council for Foreign Relations.[10] Chinese literature devoted to the topic gives a similarly negative report.[11] Little progress is to be expected in terms of giving coherence and unity of purpose to the disparate policies of various EU member states: indeed, as China rises further, the temptation will be even stronger for national governments to kowtow to Beijing.

However, the European states and the EU bodies will increasingly be forced to decide how to balance their initiatives vis-à-vis China with the value attributed to the US–European relationship. A clear example of this occurred in 2004 when certain EU member states, notably France and Italy, sought to lift the EU arms embargo imposed after the 1989 Tiananmen Square massacre. Aside from the obstacle presented by the requirement of unanimous consent, Paris and Rome rapidly encountered increasingly strong American opposition. At the end of the day, even the defence-industry lobbyists who had been pushing for the lifting of the embargo recommended a more or less graceful retreat, since it became clear that the US would severely restrict European access to US critical technology transfers and to the American aerospace market. This type of choice will be encountered more frequently and will become more contentious as China's growth as a marketplace for high technology continues: there are already more Internet connections and mobile telephones in China than in the US.

If the EU were a state, it could attempt to strike a basic bargain with the US over how to deal with a rising China, while neither harming specific European interests nor taking a military stake in East Asia (given the EU's lack of capabilities). For example, in strategic affairs, if the Europeans explicitly recognised and supported (without undermining) America's strategic role in the Asia-Pacific region, the Americans might in return provide some insight into their policies and intentions. In monetary affairs there is much to be gained by coordinating US and European policy on the renminbi exchange rate. The EU and the US could also work together upstream, and *with* China downstream, in environmental matters. The opposite happened at Copenhagen, leaving the EU up the creek without a paddle. In the meantime, China will offer assorted blandishments and punishments (the latter whenever Tibet or Taiwan are on the agenda) to the individual member states of the EU, while making little secret of the limited weight Beijing attributes to the Europeans collectively. It is only when traditional tools of power are wielded by certain states (i.e. France and the UK as permanent members of the Security Council) that a degree of influence can be obtained, as was the case during the Iraq crisis or more recently towards the Iranian nuclear programme. The Europeans would also be wise not to forget that they will in one form or another have to pay a price for what the European powers did to China when it was weak, from the First Opium War (1839–42) to the looting of the Summer Palace in 1860, and the crushing of the Boxer Rebellion (1900–01). In this sense, the Europeans are in a position closer to that of a deeply reviled Japan than to that of the US, which has a less negative image, thanks to America's legacy as a promoter of republicanism and of political and economic liberalism in pre-communist China. In summary, there exist few ingredients for a step-change in the quality of EU–China relations, even if the frequency and depth of our interactions will increase as China attains super-power status.

Grand bargain with Russia

The prognosis concerning EU–Russian relations is entirely different, notwithstanding a disappointing track record. After the chaotic 1990s, Russia built a neo-Tsarist narrative, with Russia as both a Eurasian power, with a restored strategic position and great-power ambitions, driven by a semi-authoritarian government (what it terms a 'sovereign democracy'), and an economy based on the export of raw materials, notably of oil and gas, of which it is the world's largest producer. This narrative culminated with then-president Vladimir Putin's bluntly confident security-policy speech in Munich in 2007, in which he made it clear Russia was back as a world power well attuned to the exercise of raw power.[12] The apparently unceasing rise in oil and gas prices filling the coffers of a rapidly growing Russian economy and budget, an apparently successful end to the war in Chechnya (while the US was floundering in Iraq), the vigorous reining-in of politically minded oligarchs, the largely uncontested muzzling of civil society by a popular Putin and the Kremlin's 'vertical of power': all of these led to a reinvigorated sense of alienation and even threat for Russia's neighbours, including those which had joined the European Union in 2004 and 2007.

During most of that decade, the chances of developing a coherent, long-term EU-wide strategy towards Russia were minimal: if Russia's policies and governance were widely disliked, they were not generally perceived as the sort of existential military and political threat which had led to a countervailing unity of purpose during the Cold War. Indeed, the only moment when the EU came to a consensus was in 2008 when Russia invaded Georgia. Energy-supply issues did not serve to unite the Europeans, with widely different levels of dependence, and no less contrasted attitudes. A few years later, many of the obstacles to a constructive EU–Russia relationship have diminished. Russia has undergone a traumatic loss of revenue and power as a consequence of the fall in prices and demand for its hydrocarbons following the global financial crisis. Although the shock has not been as bad as the one that brought the Soviet Union's exchequer to its knees from 1986 onward, it has served as a useful reminder that dependence on raw-materials exports can, and does, cut both ways. Russian policy elites have at least tentatively come to the conclusion that economic diversification and modernisation are a matter of urgency.[13] The post-Soviet generation of leaders and analysts tends to have a good understanding of the conditions under which *modernisatsia* can occur: entrepreneurial freedom, the rule of law, unfettered access to global markets and technology. This in turn has led to a push for a foreign and security policy that is conducive to such aims.[14] The sterile pleasures of playing the Euro-Atlantic countries against each other appear to be giving way to a Russian version of Deng Xiao-ping's status-quo policy from 1979 onwards, or Turkey's present 'zero problems' foreign policy.[15] The early part of 2010 was marked inter alia by: the nuclear-arms agreement with Washington; the settlement of the long-standing maritime dispute with Norway concerning the Barents Sea, which was settled in September 2010; the new policy of empathy towards Poland; and, more contentiously, the long-term agreement with Ukraine.

Although it remains to be seen how this shift will fare during the forthcoming Russian presidential campaign – more than a little resistance will come from the *siloviki* (security, intelligence and law-enforcement officials) running the power ministries in the Kremlin – there is clearly an opportunity for the EU. The good news here is that Russia's new-found policy with its European neighbours in combination with a much less stressful and less divisive energy situation coincides with a period of development for the European Commission's energy policy. The fact that Russia is an EU neighbour could become part of the solution, playing to the EU's strengths in terms of power and influence. Visa regimes, World Trade Organisation membership, access to the various facets of the emerging EU-wide energy market and technology-transfer regimes are tools which can and should be wielded in an integrated manner by the Commission, the Council and the External Action Service. The real test here will be whether Russia accepts that it must abandon post-imperial claims on Ukraine, Belarus and Moldova, and whether it will refrain from the use of force beyond its internationally recognised borders, notably in the Southern Caucasus.

In other words, the EU and the members of the Atlantic Alliance should be thinking of striking a 'grand bargain' with Russia, sooner rather than later. The prize in strategic terms is the prospect of stabilised relations with Russia. In geo-economic terms, the EU would benefit from a very substantial hinterland, as a market for its products and services but also, if *modernisatsia* takes hold, as a platform for industrial production closer to home (in every way) than the present delocalisation of activity to Asia. For Russia, the alternative of turning towards China has rather less strategic and political appeal than a combination with the EU. A European grand bargain may fail – the history of Russia is littered with failed or counterproductive modernisations – but there is little to be lost in trying.

The Japanese 'mirror on the wall'

Japan has a number of features in common with the EU when it comes to power relations: it not only punches well below its weight but its weight is diminishing. Japan can therefore be portrayed as a mirror on the wall, which reflects not only the EU's present but possibly also its future. In diplomatic terms, Japan is the least Bismarckian of the major powers. Ever since the

Empire's defeat in 1945, Japan has been a soft-power player. In strategic terms, it is an annex of the United States. Like Europe, it sees itself as possessing an economic and social model quite distinct from the American one. Like the European model, and unlike the American Dream, this feature is not bankable on a major scale in terms of international influence. Like the EU and its members, Japan makes a substantial effort in the field of development assistance, making $9.5bn in payments in 2009 alone, according to figures from the Organisation for Economic Cooperation and Development's Development Assistance Committee (OECD-DAC), but this does not translate into visible political advantage.[16] Chinese opposition means Japan does not have a permanent seat on the Security Council. Although it has sent troops to Iraq and anti-pirate ships off the coast of Somalia, what Japan thinks, says or does about most issues of global concern usually registers rather low on the scale of strategic or diplomatic resonance.

Despite having built up the world's second-biggest economy and spending as much on its defence as the major European powers, Japan has arguably become the least 'major' of the major powers. This is not necessarily a problem from the Japanese standpoint, even if the Ministry for Foreign Affairs has worked very hard for Security Council reform: having one's security guaranteed by the US at limited cost while being seen as a trouble-free and constructive member of the international community may be rather unexciting, but it is an acceptable situation after the disastrous activity of the twentieth century. Economically, Japan has been stagnating for the last 20 years. In 2009, nominal GDP was at the level of 1989, on the eve of the bursting of the bubble. At the time of writing, the Nikkei stands at 26% of its value on the last working day of 1989. Japan is the world's oldest country in demographic terms, and given its staunch refusal to accommodate substantial flows of immigrants, its population has begun to shrink from its 2007 peak of close to 128m. It remains to be seen how such an extreme combination of strategic dependency and societal stagnation (not to mention the parlous state of public finances) will play out in a rapidly changing regional environment, marked by the rise of China, and further down the road, the prospective reunification of its former colony Korea.

This reminder serves a two fold purpose. The first is to call for a closer monitoring and understanding of developments in Japan and between Japan and its neighbours, since its fate is key to the future stability of East Asia, a vital concern for Europe's own well-being The other is to pay due heed to Japan as to other significant partners, but without expectations of a relational breakthrough. Japan is not, in effect, a global player even if its economic importance and technological proficiency make it a sectorally important factor, both as a partner and as a competitor. In the current decade and beyond, Japan's attentions will tend to be fixated on its own growing problems (the swelling, super-sized public debt and ageing population), and on its region. EU–Japanese relations deserve to be nurtured, but this need not be considered an EU priority.

Incredible India and the invisible EU

As disjointed as the EU relationship with China may be, at least there is a generally shared perception that China is incredibly important economically, environmentally and strategically. The same cannot be said of India, despite its economic prowess and acquisition of nuclear weapons. The EU, in all of its incarnations, should deliberately seek to give a prominence to its relationship with India similar to that bestowed on China. There are a number of compelling reasons for this.

Although India is still lagging at least a decade behind China in terms of GDP and foreign trade, it has been on a steadily increasing growth path, rising from an average of less than 4% in the early 1990s to more than 7% in the latter half of the 2000s.[17] Like China, it has coped well with the global financial crisis, with an 8% growth forecast for 2010 and 2011. It has faces similar demographic problems to China (a lopsided boy/girl ratio), but it will not suffer the same shock that China will experience after 2025, when up to 28% of the population will be aged 55 or over.[18] At around that time, India's comparatively more youthful population will pull ahead of China's. Despite the crippling poverty of its first decades and the stifling effects of the socialist policy pursued by its first prime minister, Jawaharlal Nehru, from 1947 to 1964, and the bureaucratic legacy of the colonial era, India has also proven remarkably resilient and stable: it has seen no Great Leaps Forward nor Cultural Revolutions, but a robust if raucous democracy and a sturdy federalism encompassing a patchwork of cultures, religions and languages. Now that India's rapidly growing economy has overtaken that of Germany in purchasing power (some $3.5 trillion for India in 2009 according to the IMF), the EU should assume that less than 20 years down the road, India will be more powerful than China is today.[19] This gives some time to think through the future relationship and to develop it jointly, rather than waiting for India to accede to the sort of term-setting position that China enjoys today.

India, like the EU, is a strongly oceanic and historically extrovert power, unlike the more continentally and regionally focused Middle Empire. Although China will be developing global naval reach, it will do so from waters where the US's strategic interests and capabilities are paramount, and the Europeans are essentially absent. India, for its part, will be the dominant naval power in the Indian Ocean, from the oil-rich but precarious Persian Gulf to the Straits of Malacca. These are waters in which the Europeans have a presence, including in the 'pure' EU format of the anti-piracy mission *Operation Atalanta*, as well as the American and Chinese navies. The Indian diaspora in the Persian Gulf is not simply an important geo-economic fact, with close to 3m Indian nationals toiling in the petro-monarchies of Kuwait, Bahrain, Qatar, the UAE and Oman where they represent a fifth of the aggregate population. Indian nationals are the largest single component of the population of the UAE.[20] This will make India a major strategic stakeholder in the Gulf, above and beyond the military or energy-import criteria which India shares in the region with the US, the Europeans and China.

The fact that India is a democracy should normally be a help rather than a hindrance in reinforcing the EU–India relationship: elites in India have enormous experience with messy, federal structures and arcane bureaucracies. However, the starting point is very low indeed, and seen as such by prominent analysts.[21] Since the External Action Service has the opportunity of adjusting the size and the quality of its presence in the world according to perceived priorities, a good place to start would be in making the New Delhi EU representation one of the four politically strongest in the world, along with Washington, Beijing and Moscow.

Brazil: the future is now?

Ever since the first Huguenot settlement in the bay of Rio de Janeiro came to an unhappy end in the 1550s, Brazil has been a land of boom and bust rather than of steady ascent to great-power status.[22] Notwithstanding its continued reliance on commodity exports and its extreme regional disparities and social inequalities, Brazil's political and economic governance appears to have broken with past malpractice and instability, while the economic base has undergone substantial diversification. As shown in Table 3, Brazil is also becoming a big player in

Table 3: **Defence Spending ($bn)**

USA	693
European Union	*259*
China	83–114
Russia	86
UK	62
Japan	52
France	48
Germany	46
Saudi Arabia	41
India	36
Brazil	30

Source: *The Military Balance 2010*, IISS, London, 2010

the field of defence. Its recent initiative with Turkey towards the Iranian nuclear dossier may have been misguided and naive: but it showed that Brazil wants to act as the major power that it is becoming. Brazil's political influence as a leading nation of the non-Western world is substantial, notably in the important and sensitive fields of nuclear non-proliferation and the uses of nuclear energy, a role enhanced by the fact that unlike India, Brazil is a member in good standing of the nuclear non-proliferation regime. If one adds to that the democratic nature of Brazil, the existence of strong economic and trade links with the EU (which is Brazil's largest trading partner), a shared language and an old and not too unhappy colonial experience with Portugal, it is not surprising that EU–Brazil relations are reasonably well developed, directly or via dedicated multilateral mechanisms (EU–Latin America meetings, EU–Mercosul gatherings, Ibero-American summits). Individual member states, most recently France, have been investing considerable energy into their economic, political, environmental and defence dialogue with Brazil.

So all is well, and the only recommendation would be to further develop a promising EU–Brazilian relationship? Although the basic answer is 'yes', a caveat is in order (which also applies, but in varying degrees to relations with other major powers). Brazil accounts for about half of South America's population, GDP and territory, and shares a border with ten out of 12 of the continent's other countries: in geopolitical terms, such a situation can lead to hegemony, benign or not so benign. Furthermore, the imbalance is stark but not enough to make such hegemony unassailable: indeed, the historical record between Brazil and Argentina (South America's second largest and strongest country) had been one of strategic competition from the colonial era until the 1980s. This entails careful handling of relations with the great power on one hand and with lesser regional players on the other: striking the right balance between bilateral and multilateral relations is a major component of such prudence.

A step-change we can believe in?

In many ways, the advice to the EU is to conserve those relationships it has, while acknowledging those that it needs to cultivate in the near future. As US power is increasingly offset by emerging centres of power, the EU would do well to stick with its oldest ally. It should not wait for the realignment of power relations, however; rather, it should intensify its links with a rising China, while remaining clear-eyed about its ability to influence Beijing. With Russia, it must use its soft-power status to push for a grand bargain. Consolidation is the key with Brazil, although Europe should be mindful of the balance of regional power in South America. With regard to India, the EU should establish a first-order relationship, which will entail a significant upgrade of its resources in that country. The suggestions for developing the EU's relations with great powers take into account the Union as it is today, while considering as a given the *prima facie* institutional changes contained in the Lisbon Treaty, notably the establishment of the External Action Service, and the decision to bring together the Commission's external-relations and foreign-aid assets with those of the Council-based CFSP/CSDP machinery.

However, these recommendations would need to be revised if the EU acquired a central role in the production of foreign and security policy in Europe. It would notably become conceivable to move towards a 'between equals–broad spectrum' relationship between Europe collectively and the US and to establish a relationship with the major powers in which the EU would represent more than the sum of its disparate parts. Therefore, the possibility of such a step-change has to be at least briefly considered, with two major agents of change being involved: the consequences of the Lisbon Treaty and the impact of the global financial crisis on the governance of the EU. The office of High Representative as established by the Lisbon Treaty, with access to substantial budget resources and control of a large diplomatic corps, certainly has the potential for gaining progressively a greater role in the upstream formulation of foreign and security policy. By making it clear that the full weight of EU capabilities would be more readily mobilised in this way, the High Representative could gradually build up influence. In situations in which member states, for reasons of their own, would be standing aside, a heavyweight HR could be tempted to take the lead. An increasingly influential HR may be on the cards, but the office is unlikely to become more autonomous and powerful: member states remain, under the Lisbon Treaty, the fountainhead of foreign and security policy decision-making, and they will be loath to allow that situation to be changed. This does not mean that there never will exist in the foreign and security policy field the functional equivalent of the single currency, with its abandonment of a broad swath of national sovereignty. Simply, as in the case of the euro, this will entail new treaty commitments.

Could the solidarity clause of the Lisbon Treaty (Article 222) provide a foundation for a step change?[23] In a maximalist reading, the clause could provide the basis for the creation of the EU equivalent of NATO's Supreme Allied Commander of Europe (SACEUR) and the permanent earmarking of troops to the EU; and as in the Atlantic Alliance, an EU defence capability could move over time into the realm of far-flung expeditionary warfare. However, that was not the intent of those who drafted the treaty, and the clause's multifaceted language reflects the multiplicity of views rather than an underlying unity of purpose. A complete change of the EU's security situation, combining a deep estrangement from the US with a brutally clear and present military danger specifically aimed at the EU and its members, would be necessary to create this kind of transformation.

The economic and financial crisis of 2008–09 is another very serious matter which has led the EU and its member states to revisit the issue of economic governance and of the obligations (or the lack thereof) of the member states in terms of financial solidarity and budgetary discipline. The tensions generated within the EU and the eurozone remain unresolved at the time of writing. The European integration process has moved forward through a series of crises – the non-ratification of the European Defence Community in 1954, de Gaulle's empty-chair policy in the mid-1960s, Margaret Thatcher's successful demands for a budget rebate for the UK in 1984 and the non-ratification of the Constitutional Treaty by France and the Netherlands in 2005, to mention but a few. Given the scale of the current crisis, one could therefore expect a step-change, at least in the field of economic and political governance. This could include, for instance, a mandatory stability pact policed by the Commission within the eurozone, and Council-level economic governance under which member states would introduce German-style primary budget ceilings within their national constitutions. In the past, such moves towards an 'ever closer union among the peoples of Europe' have tended to spill over into other areas: for example, the long march towards the euro and the birth of the European Security and Defence Policy (now the CSDP) occurred in parallel, in part because Britain's absence from the euro prompted the New Labour government under Tony Blair to find another way of being at 'the heart of Europe'.[24] Conversely, a failure to develop EU economic governance in a situation of monetary and economic entropy could also occur, in which case the opposite effect would presumably prevail. In the meantime, the EU possesses its specific set of tools, its *sui generis* organisational culture, its complex institutional characteristics. It is on the basis of such realities that relations with the major powers should be considered.

CHAPTER TWO

Military and Civilian Capabilities for EU-led Crisis-Management Operations

Bastian Giegerich

Consulting Senior Fellow for European Security, IISS, and Senior Researcher at the Bundeswehr Institute of Social Sciences, Germany

When EU member states initiated the European Security and Defence Policy (ESDP, since 1 December 2009 known as the Common Security and Defence Policy, [CSDP]) in 1999, a major goal was to improve European capabilities for military, civilian and civil–military crisis-management missions in order to fulfil the ambition to provide capacities for autonomous EU action.[1] This in turn would help the EU to live up to its self-declared aspiration of being a global security actor. More than ten years on, this goal has only been partially met.

EU documents acknowledge that with a view to 2010, the Union 'has the capability to conduct the full spectrum of military operations within the parameters of the Strategic Planning Assumptions, with different levels of operational risks arising from the identified shortfalls'.[2] Stripped of jargon, this phrase means that despite considerable efforts spanning the past decade, significant military capability gaps continue to exist if judged against the spectrum of operations the EU wants to be able to conduct.[3]

The problem is widely recognised. The former EU high representative for Common Foreign and Security Policy (CFSP),

Javier Solana, remarked in 2009: 'Our ambitions are growing, not diminishing. However, there is a gap between our ambitions and the reality of our capabilities.'[4] Nick Witney, the former chief executive of the European Defence Agency, was less forgiving in his appraisal: 'EU leaders commit to ambitious defence goals and deadlines, celebrate inadequate outcomes, move the goalposts, and authorise a further round of "reviews" and "roadmaps".'[5]

The reasons for this unsatisfactory state of affairs are manifold. One has to take into account that all decisions with regards to capability development and capability provision are still being taken at the national and not at the EU level. This implies that implementation problems with regard to capability goals in the military and civilian sphere have to be located mostly in the capitals of member states and not so much within the EU institutions. Shrinking defence expenditure, inertia created by structurally conservative bureaucracies, factors such as geographic location, strategic culture and threat perceptions, as well as expectations of external actors and current operational experiences, are variables that help to explain the different national positions. It is perhaps not surprising that collectively defined goals, be they within the EU or NATO, have only limited influence in this complex web of international and domestic determinants of national policy.

Capability development processes

In general, the processes for military and civilian capability development within the CSDP are similar; however, until now they have remained relatively uncoordinated.[6] In the military realm, the process starts with the definition of illustrative scenarios which, on the basis of parameters – such as the duration of a mission, rotation requirements, required readiness levels and distance to the theatre of operation – describe the different types of missions that fall within the CSDP's competence. At present, the EU is using five military scenario 'families' based on different Strategic Planning Assumptions. On the basis of these planning assumptions, one then defines which capabilities would be necessary to conduct a certain operation. All of this planning work leads to the so-called Requirements Catalogue. Once this catalogue is defined, EU member states are invited to pledge their contributions according to the list of capabilities contained within it. Pledges from member-state governments are then combined in a so-called Force Catalogue, which defines and describes what has been pledged by member states. By comparing the two catalogues, it is possible to identify the capability gaps or shortfalls. These exist either because member states do not possess the necessary capabilities, or because they do not make them available to the EU. The list of capability gaps and their implications for potential CSDP operations are then brought together in yet another catalogue misleadingly called the Progress Catalogue. The corresponding scenarios on the civilian side were developed independently of the military side in 2005. They provide the basis for defining the required tasks and corresponding personnel. Similar to the preparation for the military field, member states pledge contributions, which are then compared to the requirements.

Military capabilities

The European Council meeting in Helsinki in December 1999 defined what came to be known as the Helsinki Headline Goal, a military capabilities goal member states tried to implement by the end of 2003. It said:

> By the year 2003, cooperating together voluntarily [the EU member states] will be able to deploy rapidly and then sustain forces capable of the full range of

the Petersberg[7] tasks as set out in the Amsterdam Treaty, including the most demanding, in operations up to corps level (up to 15 brigades or 50,000–60,000 persons).[8]

It is no secret that experiences, including those in Kosovo, had a strong influence on the definition of the headline goal – in essence, it outlined the aspiration of being able to conduct an operation up to corps level without relying on US capabilities. However, 2003 came and went, and even though it was obvious that significant capability gaps persisted, member states presented a new goal in May 2004, the Headline Goal 2010. EU member governments committed themselves to being able 'to respond with rapid and decisive action applying a fully coherent approach to the whole spectrum of crisis management operations covered by the Treaty on the European Union'.[9] Even though member states were more than equal to attaining the corps target of the original headline goal, they still did not possess capabilities that would enable the more demanding operations at the upper end of the Petersberg task spectrum.

To mitigate this, the *European Capabilities Action Plan* (ECAP) had been created in 2001. This programme comprised 19 project groups, each working on a specific capability area under the guidance of a lead nation, which were supposed to help EU member states reach their capability goals. The whole process was based on voluntary commitments from member states. It emerged, however, that the logic of voluntary bottom-up co-operation had severe limitations. The EU's Political and Security Committee (PSC) argued: 'some adjustment of ECAP would be needed to bridge the gap between the voluntary basis on which ECAP Project Groups ... operate and the interest of the Union as a whole to acquire all military capabilities needed'.[10] In other words, the voluntary cooperation process did not yield the necessary results. Member governments continued to make decisions based purely on national considerations and thus did not contribute to problem-solving in the form of capability generation through multinational processes such as ECAP. In this context, the creation of the European Defence Agency (EDA) in 2004 was an important step. As the Council clarified, the main goal of the agency is 'to deliver the military capabilities that CSDP requires'.[11]

Correspondingly, the EDA has published a series of strategy documents which help to define which capabilities and technologies are needed and what kind of cooperation should be established so that progress can be made on building capability. The Capability Development Plan (CDP) of July 2008 is noteworthy in this regard. It aims to provide information to member-state governments which should facilitate national decision-making. For example, governments could use the CDP to find which government in the EU is working on priorities or projects similar to their own. The assumption is that this kind of information sharing would foster cooperation and generate new projects. The CDP is scheduled to be updated by the end of 2010, at which time important initiatives for collaboration should be identified.

The need for initiatives is clear, because progress has been slow. In 2002, the EU had defined 64 capability deficits. A report in mid-2006 showed that only seven of those problems had been solved, with another four areas described as making progress.[12] This means that across 53 areas, nothing much had changed in four years. Interestingly enough, the EU stopped publishing these half-yearly reports in 2006, presumably because they merely underlined publicly the lack of progress.

It seems clear than that CSDP has not been successful in developing better military capabilities in Europe. The core capability gaps in the areas of strategic and tactical airlift, intelligence and reconnaissance, as well as force protection, persist. To revive this topic, the French EU presidency in the second half of 2008 initiated a Declaration on Strengthening Capabilities.[13] The declaration set out in relatively clear terms what the EU's level of ambition would be for civilian and military crisis-management missions. It argued that the EU, in implementing the military and civilian Headline Goal 2010 obligations, should be able to conduct simultaneously two major stabilisation and reconstruction operations involving up to 10,000 troops plus a civilian contingent for at least two years; two rapid-response operations using EU battlegroups; an evacuation operation in less than ten days; a maritime or air surveillance/interdiction operation; a civil–military humanitarian assistance operation of up to 90 days' duration, or around a dozen civilian missions including one major operation involving up to 3,000 personnel for several years. Notably absent from this list is an operation dealing with a 'separation of parties by force' scenario. Even though such an operation falls within the EU's ambitions, persistent capabilities shortfalls seem to have precluded its inclusion.

Underlining the perceived uniqueness of the EU as a crisis-management actor and the perception that demand would increase in particular in the civilian arena, the declaration made progress on civilian capabilities a priority area. On the military side, the declaration asked member states to embrace innovative methods for capabilities development, including the pooling and multinational management of assets, role specialisation for rare and costly niche capabilities, and the collective procurement of critical capabilities. Pursuing such a course is understood to be one of the few remaining options to significantly improve capabilities, particularly in light of the enormous budget pressures European governments face in the wake of the economic and financial crisis of 2008–09. The need for such innovative collaboration will have to be balanced with governments' desire to maintain national security and defence priorities, since such methods invariably amount to an increase of mutual interdependence among participating countries. It is therefore likely that governments will define capability areas in which they are unwilling to collaborate, because they are deemed vital for national purposes before they move on to consider practical steps of identifying capabilities that can be shared and pooled or reflect in earnest on arrangements for role and task specialisation. The danger for the immediate future is that national governments, feeling the budgetary crunch, will make deep cuts in a manner that is not coordinated with partners, and in some cases possibly in ignorance of similar plans in partner countries, which will lead to a reduction of capabilities on the national level and a reduced ability to exploit the advantages of closer cooperation in the future. After all, reaping the benefits of cooperation assumes interoperability and a certain degree of complementarity among European militaries.

Furthermore, in the second half of 2008, and thus also under the French EU presidency, a number of project-based initiatives were started among clusters of EU member states. For example, it was decided that in the field of satellite-based reconnaissance the Italian *Cosmo Skymed* and the French *Helios* 2 satellites would provide imagery to the EU satellite centre based in Spain. Germany declared its intention to do the same with its new *SAR-Lupe* satellite system. In addition, Belgium, Germany, France, Greece and Italy decided to develop a new generation of Earth-observation satellites, the so-called MUSIS programme. The EDA is now also hosting collaborative projects in the development of mine countermeasures and unmanned aerial vehicles. More visible initiatives included the declaration by 12 EU member states in November 2008 to create a European Air Transport Fleet, to pool support functions for C-130 and in the future A400M transport planes. At the same time, nine member states created the European Carrier Group Interoperability Initiative. It tried to increase the interoperability of European navies so that participating countries will in the future find it easier to contribute to a multinational carrier group, for example, by providing escort ships. Against the background of unsatisfactory progress in the past ten years, there seems to be a trend towards more flexible forms of cooperation for capability development. Clearly, member states are trying to avoid any measures that would unduly restrict their sovereignty, given that this is an extremely sensitive area.

Civilian capabilities
In terms of public attention, civilian capabilities are often an afterthought compared to the military side. This is not surprising if one considers that the initial premise behind ESDP/CSDP was indeed military, and that military operations receive more media attention than civilian ones do. On the other hand, this imbalance obscures the fact that CSDP is explicitly concerned with combining military and civilian instruments. Furthermore, a clear majority of ongoing CSDP missions is in fact civilian (see table below). The problems of capability development in the civilian sphere are somewhat different than in the military realm. Civilian capabilities are almost always linked to specific individuals, and have a lot less to do with platforms and equipment. The biggest problem in the civilian sphere is the enormous gap between existing, pledged and deployed personnel.[14]

Capabilities development in the civilian field started in 2000, when four priority areas were defined: police, rule of law, civil administration and civil protection. Again, numerical targets were set by EU member states. A civilian headline goal, defined in 2004, added new priority areas, namely monitoring and support for EU special representatives, with attainment expected after four years. The Civilian Headline Goal 2008, which member states try to fulfil by pursuing national action plans, further defined the aspiration of being able to conduct several civilian CSDP missions simultaneously. Around 18,000 civilian personnel would be required to implement the five operations to be conducted simultaneously under the headline goals. In the Civilian Headline Goal 2008, the EU already acknowledged shortfalls in the numbers of judges and prosecutors, police and border control staff. However, the lists for the civilian headline goals were drawn up at a time when the real-world demands on civilian CSDP missions were not yet fully understood – shortfalls in operational experience therefore make the Civilian Headline Goal 2008 a mostly theoretical exercise. A successor, the Civilian Headline Goal 2010, was defined as early as 2007. It called for improved planning capacity for simultaneous missions, for better training of civilian personnel on international deployments and for national strategies promoting the exchange of best practices. It also stressed the importance of rapidly deployable police units, improved information sharing and intelligence cooperation.

The EU's strength, in terms of civilian capabilities, lies in its ability to coordinate civilian resources from 27 states. However, this advantage also creates several problems. For example, unlike soldiers, civilians cannot simply be ordered to participate in international missions; volunteers have to be recruited, which can make it difficult to fill the necessary slots, not least because of the lack of professional benefits civilian personnel can gain by signing up for foreign missions. In addition, the individuals in question are most likely already doing their job in a national setting, which means that their international deployment creates a vacancy at home that would need to be filled. This can lead to reduced pledges by EU member states.

A serious problem is that EU member states pursue very different strategies when it comes to civilian capability generation and provision, with significant consequences for both quantity and quality of personnel. As a 2009 audit of civilian capabilities across EU nations revealed, some member-state governments provide in-depth training and dedicated planning structures; they organise mandatory debriefings of deployed personnel and have instituted 'lessons learned' processes. Others, however, do very little of this. As the authors of the review argued, the EU struggles to 'transform what are currently ad hoc and disjointed national efforts into a more systematic pan-European endeavour'.[15]

Furthermore, acquisition processes in the civilian field have not yet been adapted to the realities of international crisis-management missions. What might be considered an acceptable lag between the ordering and delivery of office furniture in Brussels is not necessarily feasible on operations. Finally, responsibility for the different aspects of civilian capabilities is divided among many institutions in EU member states, which on the one hand creates an additional burden in terms of coordination, and on the other implies that personnel will have different levels of training. These differences cannot simply be adapted through targeted pre-deployment training even if such training covers similar skill sets. Correspondingly, the areas of personnel, logistics and planning have already proven to be problematic in the reality of CSDP missions.

CSDP operations

Since 2003 the EU has launched 24 CSDP operations. While these endeavours demonstrate a certain shared will to engage, the flurry of activity should not be mistaken for progress. CSDP operations cover an increasing geographical and functional scope (see table below) but they are often rather limited in size and their impact on the crisis situation at hand is often unclear. Furthermore, it is not possible to discern clear criteria upon which decisions to launch an operation are based. Most of the time the EU is reactive rather than proactive, driven by either external demands, specific interests of a member state, or the sheer desire to demonstrate a capacity for action. The fact that five of the EU's missions took place in the Democratic Republic of the Congo (DRC), for example, seems to be due to French interests, UN requests and the desire to show that the CSDP had entered the real, operational world. None of those are bad reasons for engagement per se, but they fall short of the preventive character the EU aspires to and demonstrate a lack of strategic planning. Some governments within the EU resent the impression that an EU label is attached to what are essentially priorities of a single member state, whereas actors outside the EU question the neutrality of EU action in cases where postcolonial ties are perceived to be among the reasons for engagement. The results are tightly defined and risk-averse EU mandates, because of the need to balance different member states' interests and the desire to maintain international legitimacy. As the table also shows, much of EU action takes place in the civilian realm, and while there are a number of military missions, *integrated* civilian–military operations where the EU supposedly could add most value are so far virtually non-existent.

A recent review of all EU missions conducted up to the second half of 2009 argued that operational mandates, the resources made available by member states, the degree to which operations were pursued in a framework that combined civilian and military means, and the political context and security situation in a given crisis area together determined how successful operations were. For example, EUPOL Afghanistan was hampered by a mandate that never accounted for the

Table 1: **CSDP Operations 2003–2010**

	Civilian	Civilian–Military	Military
Completed	EUPOL *Proxima* FYROM 2004–2005	Support to AMIS II Sudan/Darfur 2005–2006	*Concordia* FYROM 2003
	EUPAT FYROM 2006		*Artemis* RD Congo 2003
	EUJUST *Themis* Georgia 2004–2005		EUFOR RD Congo RD Congo 2006
	EUPOL Kinshasa RD Congo 2005–2007		EUFOR Tchad/RCA Tchad/RCA 2008–2009
	AMM Monitoring Mission Aceh/Indonesia 2005–2006		
Ongoing	EUPM Bosnia-Hercegovina Since 2003 Strength: 284		EUFOR *Althea* Bosnia-Hercegovina Since 2004 Strength: 1,950
	EULEX Kosovo Kosovo Since 2008 Strength: 2,764		EUNAVFOR *Atalanta* Since 2008 Strength: 1,144
	EUBAM Moldova and Ukraine Since 2005 Strength: 200		EUTM Somalia Somalia/Uganda Since 2010 Strength: 118
	EUMM Georgia Georgia Since 2008 Strength: 405		
	EUPOL COPPS Palestine Since 2006 Strength: 85		
	EUPOL Afghanistan Afghanistan Since 2007 Strength: 459		
	EU SSR Guinea Bissau Guinea Bissau Since 2008 Strength: 24		
	EUBAM Rafah Palestine Since 2005 Strength: 21		
	EUJUST LEX Iraq/Brussels Since 2005 Strength: 42		
	EUSEC RD Congo RD Congo Since 2005 Strength: 44		
	EUPOL RD Congo RD Congo Since 2007 Strength: 60		

Personnel numbers as of July 2010. Figures include local staff. Source: European Union deteriorating security situation and did not provide enough equipment or personnel to meet the country's increasing needs. Even those low numbers of personnel foreseen were not met through member-state contributions. By July 2010, EUPOL had a strength of some 285 deployed personnel against an authorised strength of 400. EULEX Kosovo struggled, among other reasons, because not all EU member states recognised Kosovo's independence; the unclear legal status provided an awkward political background for the mission. In the Palestinian territory police and border-assistance missions have become a political football in the power struggle between Hamas and Fatah. The border-assistance mission in Rafah in the Gaza Strip has been suspended since June 2007 as a result of Hamas taking over the border crossing. The monitoring mission in Georgia, which is tasked with monitoring the implementation of the 12 August and 8 September 2008 agreements that ended hostilities between Russia and Georgia, has still not gained access to the disputed territories of South Ossetia and Abkhazia, even though the EUMM mandate covers all of Georgia's territory within its internationally recognised borders.[16]

The EU's Institute for Security Studies published a 'lessons learned' document on the EUFOR Tchad/RCA operation of 2008–09.[17] The document is instructive because it demonstrates that many problems that emerged during military operations in the DRC in 2003 and again in 2006 remain unresolved. While EU–UN cooperation had improved, both institutions still pursued very different operational priorities. Whereas the EU intended to focus on the security of internally displaced persons, leading to an operational focus on the southern part of the area of operations, UN planning focused on refugees located in the northern part of the area of operations. However, following the end of the EU operation, many of its troops re-hatted under the UN mission, thus providing important capability for the UN. In 2003 and 2006, following the operations in the DRC, EU member states chose not to do so, causing a drop in international capability in the theatre of operations.

EUFOR Tchad/RCA saw again the involvement of third parties. For example, Russian helicopters were included to provide much needed tactical-airlift capability. While the use of such assets is encouraging and provides a good example of constructive collaboration, the fact that it took nine months to deploy these helicopters – in part because a drawn-out negotiation was needed to set up planning and liaison procedures between Russia and the EU – points to the need to establish permanent framework agreements for such instances.

In another parallel to the DRC operations, the high number of contributor nations in Tchad/RCA, most of them with relatively small contingents, made logistics overly complex. It also meant that operations were driven by the need to meet a predetermined end date and thus followed a political logic that had little to do with the actual situation on the ground. Thus, again, the EU had successfully conducted a military operation in Africa in support of the UN, at least when judged against the mandate that the military was given by its political masters. Overall, *Artemis* in the DRC in 2003, EUFOR RD Congo in 2006 and EUFOR Tchad/RCA were limited operations that produced results within the limited parameters of what they set out to do. From a political point of view, their main achievement was symbolic: they demonstrated the EU capacity for action in general and, specifically, in support of the UN. While this kind of achievement builds confidence and adds to the body of shared CSDP experience among EU member states, the long-term impact of the missions on peace and stability in the respective crisis areas is less clear.

Given the strength of the narrative that depicts the EU as a civilian power, albeit one with a military capability, it is more disturbing that general assessments of civilian operations seem to come to the conclusion that the EU's civilian efforts are less successful than their military counterparts. One report argues: 'the EU's supposed civilian power is largely illusory ... [Even] when the EU does manage to sustain a significant [civilian] mission abroad, the results are often paltry.'[18] The operational record thus does not point to an obvious comparative advantage of the EU: both civilian and military operations were conducted with mixed results. Military operations seem to benefit from the armed forces' ability to implement the mandates given to them by political leaders. But by and large operations so far have been of limited strategic value – in terms of having a lasting impact – and truly integrated civilian–military operations have not even been attempted at this point.

The limits of bottom-up collaboration on capabilities

The core problems remain the ever-increasing operational demands on military and civilian personnel on operations, the persistent gaps as yet not filled by the capability development processes in the EU, and the enormous cost pressure. In the future there will even be less money available, in particular with regard to defence. Thus, the basic principle which so far has driven capabilities development, namely voluntary bottom-up cooperation, seems to have reached its limits. Overall, one can conclude that most of the operations the EU wants to be able to conduct can be undertaken on the basis of existing capabilities. However, to fulfil the self-defined aspiration of being a global security actor, the gap has to be closed. Particularly in the context of ever increasing financial and resource pressures, it seems likely that the only way to do so is by increasing levels of cooperation among member states. Especially in the military realm, one can see the possibility that flexible small groups of EU member states might band together to advance capabilities development. Of course, CSDP is based on the principles of unanimity and equality of member states. Instruments of informal cooperation will have to take the consensual nature of CSDP into account and those member states willing and able to lead will have to undertake considerable efforts to avoid giving the impression that they are passing over the views of their fellow EU member governments.

It is telling that great uncertainty surrounds the permanent structured cooperation on defence (PSCD), an instrument introduced in 2009 under the Lisbon Treaty to facilitate more effective processes of capabilities development for crisis-management operations. The PSCD allows member states 'whose military capabilities fulfil higher criteria and which have made binding commitments to one another ... with a view to the most demanding operations' to set up a leadership group seeking closer cooperation, but within the EU framework. The underlying rationale for such a procedure should be to generate relevant and useable capabilities at greater financial efficiency for EU operations. However, when discussions on how to implement this treaty provision took place during the first half of 2010, it seemed as if member states were far from agreement on whether the process was even feasible, much less convinced on the detail of the process.

A key division stems from the problem that the PSCD is seen by several governments as a means to foster closer cooperation on defence among member states in principle and thus, those governments argue, it needs to be as inclusive as possible, ideally involving all member states. Such a perspective runs counter to the argument advanced by others that the PSCD should only be open to those EU members who are willing and able to make the necessary commitments and actually generate better capabilities, which would entail a more selective approach to who is allowed to participate. There is no consensus regarding what kind of criteria should be applied, which is largely a result of the fact that no consensus exists with regard to the PSCD's main function. Because the PSCD threatens to become an unwieldy and overly complex process in the absence of a harmonised understanding of what it is supposed to achieve, several governments have begun to argue that, at least for the time being, this treaty provision should not be activated.

A core question arising from this is whether political legitimacy can be balanced with effectiveness. In others words, do EU member states want a process that is inclusive and hence fairly legitimate, but one that might fail to deliver? Or do leaders prefer a process that is better at delivering capability even if it comes at the cost of inclusivity? A related question concerns the core goal of the PSCD. Is it about convergence, in other words making member states more alike, with the result being an improved set of capabilities? Or is it about enabling a leadership group of the most capable countries to go ahead and form a vanguard? In principle, the idea of a vanguard demands criteria focused on input and output of member states wishing to participate, whereas the convergence model would focus solely on output. Conceptually, the EU's mix of civilian and military instruments and the potential for integrated civilian–military operation are compelling and describe the comparative advantage of the EU as a security organisation engaged in crisis-management tasks. However, while the potential of the EU in this field is considerable, civilian and military capability generation and CSDP operations have so far yielded rather limited results.

CHAPTER THREE

The Effects of Global Demographics

Christopher Langton
Former Senior Fellow for Conflict and Defence Diplomacy, IISS

In the post-colonial era following the Second World War, people from former European colonies were introduced into the countries of the European colonial powers in large numbers. This settlement of people of different races, religions and cultures appeared initially to have been absorbed successfully into the receiving societies. In part this was due to immigrants having a common language with their former colonial rulers; at that time religion was not a contentious issue in the way it is today. However, despite some social commonality, significant proportions of minority ethnic communities were not integrated properly into the largely indigenous communities. The result was that non-integrated immigrant communities grew up in ghettos in a number of urban areas across Europe, which sowed the seeds for the problems that accompanied the next wave of immigration. Today, some of the greatest challenges to European security are to be found in the demographics of the twenty-first century. Globalisation has facilitated the movement of migrants to Europe from more areas of the world than in the colonial and post-colonial era combined. Climate change threatens to give added impetus to this changing migratory pattern, raising the possibility that tensions between immigrant and host communities may flare up.

Demographic trends

The world population is set to grow from an estimated 6.9 billion in 2010 to more than 9bn by 2050.[1] In general the shifts in the numbers of indigenous and domestic populations in Europe are complicated by the migration patterns of non-indigenous people into, and through, the region. Internal European demographic variations are therefore linked to changing demographic patterns outside the region. As an example of the scale and character of migration into Europe, the 8.7 million increase in the EU's population of between 2004 and 2007 included 1.4m migrants from the Middle East and Africa and 1m migrants from Russia and non-EU Eastern European countries.

Globalisation plays a part in changing the patterns of migration by facilitating and encouraging the mobility of migrating people from almost anywhere in the world. Thus, there is a greater mix of cultures and languages emerging within Europe than was the case after the first post-war phase of immigration. One of the most visible demographic changes is the rise in the Muslim population in a largely secular Christian Europe. The increasing diversity of cultures has the potential to cause tension and instability if it becomes imbalanced. Chancellor Angela Merkel said multiculturalism had 'failed utterly', adding that

Case Study: UK Immigration

The UK's population is 61 million today, and is forecast to reach 70m in 2028. According to Eurostat the UK will have the largest population in Europe by 2060. 70% of this growth will be due to immigration.

Net immigration has quadrupled since 1997 to 237,000 a year.

Source: Eurostat and the UK Office of National Statistics

Germans and migrant workers could not live happily side by side, in an address to her party's youth wing in October 2010. She also said that many guest workers who had been encouraged to come to Germany to help rebuild the nation after the Second World War had stayed, but had not learned to speak German. The demand for integration, the chancellor said, was one of the key tasks for the times to come.[2]

On the other hand, there are numerous examples of the positive and enriching contribution of immigrants to the receiving societies. The UK National Security Strategy 2010 said: 'Migration brings major economic benefits. In destination countries, it supports economic growth and labour market flexibility. In source countries, it generates remittances from migrant workers, which the World Bank estimates are now twice the total of global aid.'[3]

The challenge for the EU is how to absorb those immigrants that enrich European societies while controlling the growing tide of migration without compromising the human-rights principles or security of the EU. The EU is regarded as a destination of choice for migrants because of its perceived liberal border regime, economic benefits including health care, and the promise of a safer and more prosperous future. For traffickers and criminals of many types, Europe is the location of choice because of the 'market' opportunities it offers. Apart from the effects of globalisation, mobility and liberalisation, the emerging factors causing migratory pressures are in some cases non-traditional, such as the growing impact of climate change, which some experts now view as likely to lead to the increasing movements of peoples towards Europe from the east and south; although there is uncertainty over the volume of migration flows.[4] The population estimates produced by Eurostat show the birth rate is exceeding the death rate across Europe, with a decline in populations only taking place in a few countries.[5] The rise usually occurs in the immigrant rather than the domestic part of a population.

Changes in population levels range from an annual decline in 2008–09 of five per 1,000 in Bulgaria to an increase of 22 in 1,000 in Iceland. One observation from these statistics is that some notable population shifts sometimes occur in countries not previously associated with large immigrant populations such as Iceland, but also Luxembourg, Cyprus and Slovenia. On the other hand Spain, a former colonial power within reach of North Africa, has a growing, largely Muslim, immigrant community. Overall the Spanish population grew by an estimated 12.5 in 1,000 in 2008.[6]

Globally the number of people over the age of 60 is expected to rise from 739m in 2009 to 2bn in 2050,[7] putting pressure on employment, economic and fiscal policies. The majority of people in this category live in developed countries where healthcare is better than in under-developed and developing countries. Therefore, pensions to support retired workers in ageing domestic populations are a particular issue for governments and the EU. A related issue is the potentially negative effect of an ageing workforce. It is possible that a smaller and older labour force would have less ability to innovate, which would affect the competitiveness of European economies. In general, it is expected that the domestic/indigenous populations of 16 out of 27 EU member states will decline in the period to 2050.[8] This group is living longer but producing smaller families. Therefore today's domestic populations will work beyond existing retirement ages, leaving a gap at the other end of the labour market which may be filled increasingly by immigrants as a matter of necessity; especially in times of economic growth when countries need migrant labour to accelerate infrastructure projects and construction. The link between the numerical decline in domestic populations (but with ageing populations who may work longer) and the steep rise in African, Asian and other populations – some of whom may be forced into migration by the effects of climate change and poor living conditions – has yet to be determined.

While domestic populations in Europe decline, the working-age population (20 to 64 years of age) of African countries is expected to rise from the 2005 total of 408m to an estimated 1.1bn by 2050.[9] The opportunities offered to European countries by greater migrant availability may prove attractive to some governments whose domestic populations will become increasingly expensive in terms of wages and pensions, as they work longer and have fewer babies; and the pressure on European borders is likely to grow when faced with this increasing demographic challenge from African countries beset with economic and climatic difficulties. However, the idea of implementing a policy of replacement migration has been firmly rejected in Europe. Instead, most European countries hope to offset demographic decline with family-friendly policies and active-ageing measures. Most groups working on immigration (governments included) are focusing on how immigration can contribute as part of the policy mix.

With the global economic crisis affecting all European economies and the eurozone in particular, the EU must control immigration and disincentivise would-be migrants from coming to Europe or moving in large numbers within Europe. The lack of consistency between national economic opportunities and national immigration policies creates new challenges. Economic immigrants or those that have been displaced by conflict or climate are unlikely to remain in their mother countries simply because economic opportunities in European countries are fewer. Refugees from the conflicts in the Balkans in the 1990s moved freely and legally in large numbers from the conflict zones through Europe until reaching the English

Channel. They were held up by UK immigration law but still persisted in reaching the UK by illicit means. The Sangatte refugee camp near Calais was created to house these people and challenged the human-rights agenda of the European Union by its very existence. In 2010 the French government's declaration that Roma people should be repatriated also challenged EU human-rights norms but also showed where EU immigration policy remains subject to national policy.

Human-security risks

Global demographic shifts allow traditional threats such as extremism to grow and non-traditional threats to human security to emerge within Europe. The latter category includes climate change and environmental issues which may have an impact on populations in the south and east of Europe in particular.[10] These were not traditionally viewed as threats to national security, but they are increasingly treated as such by policymakers. Increasing urbanisation will bring its own problems to do with insecurity and disease.

Terror and crime

According to the International Organisation for Migration, of the 130m international migrants globally, some 20–40m are illegal, and at any one time about 4m illegal migrants are on the move. Illegal immigration into Europe has been estimated as being between 400,000 and 800,000 annually.[11] Illegal migrants are often the chosen facilitator of the criminal and non-state world, once again highlighting the increased need to control borders at a time when globalisation and the liberalisation of trade regimes challenges the idea, and the Schengen Zone of the EU is virtually free of border controls.

An increase in the number of people migrating to Europe from North and West Africa in particular raises the likelihood of continuing terrorism within Europe executed under the banner of global jihad. Global terrorism in the name of al-Qaeda (AQ) and religion has been nurtured in Europe through Islamic communities with connections to militant groups in Muslim countries. The presence of militant Islamic groups on the borders of Europe such as the Algerian Salafist Group for Preaching and Combat (GSPC), which has close links to al-Qaeda and from which al-Qaeda in the Islamic Maghreb (AQIM) was born, feeds off Muslim communities in France and Spain in particular (see Nigel Inkster's chapter on terrorism in Europe). These communities, particularly in Spain, are growing at a faster rate than the indigenous populations of the host countries; and Islam is in consequence the fastest-growing religion in Europe and may be expected to double to 40m within the next 20 years. Dissatisfaction in these communities, fuelled by violent rhetoric and imported Wahhabist ideology, motivates the disaffected, mostly young and often unemployed immigrants.[12]

Non-violent movements such as Hizb-ut-Tahrir (Party of Liberation) have grown up in this environment, spreading a largely anti-Western message and enabling the radicalisation of some of their members who may then join global jihad with AQ and AQIM. Hizb-ut-Tahrir's objectives are openly non-violent but have the proven potential to radicalise young disaffected Muslims. It is self-evident that with a growth in the number of Muslims in Europe and a decline in domestic populations, there is a risk (which should not be over-stated) of sectarian tensions rising in some of the most heavily populated European states, focused in the growth of urban communities.

The response by European countries to the various transnational and internal threats is diverse. For example, some countries have banned Hizb-ut-Tahrir, whereas others have not. This can have the effect of displacing activists from one country to another. And the different approaches of states to racism, as highlighted in the 24 June 2010 report by the EU watchdog, the Fundamental Rights Agency,[13] can also act as a displacer of immigrants who may wish to seek a better life in a country where racism is less prevalent. The rise of far-right and neo-fascist movements as one reaction to the growing number of immigrants as well as Islamic extremism is likely to continue and to challenge democratic principles. The growth in the number of Members of the European Parliament (MEPs) elected from rightist organisations bears witness to this trend and mirrors to some extent the problems faced by the EU in coming to terms with the demographic consequences of immigration. These problems are likely to become more rather than less challenging given the demographic trends of this century.

Violent nationalist and domestic criminal groups may compete with emerging groups in immigrant communities. The competition for 'territory' is likely to become acute in an increasingly multicultural, urbanised Europe. The lessons of twentieth-century New York may be re-learned in European cities. The inability of the US to assimilate illegal Italian immigrants into society led to the creation of mafia gangs, which competed violently outside the control of the state authorities with domestic Irish-American gangs. For a time they were a virtual 'state within a state' running lucrative illegal as well as legal 'front' businesses and massive trafficking operations, including heroin and cocaine from Colombian cartels. There are also lessons to be learned from the impact of urbanisation on Latin American and African cities. The 'mega-slums' of Rio, Sao Paulo and Lagos are examples which show how sheer population growth can give birth to shadow societies that are autonomous and within which criminality can exist with impunity.

Climate change and demographic patterns

A joint paper by the European Commission and the Council, presented in March 2008, stressed that the EU had to focus on the mitigation of and preparation for the inevitable effects of climate change as a part of its preventive security policy: 'Climate change is best viewed as a threat multiplier which exacerbates existing trends, tensions and instability'.[14] In 2009 the United Kingdom's National Security Strategy stated:

> climate change will increasingly be a wide-ranging driver of global insecurity. It acts as a threat-multiplier, exacerbating weakness and tensions around the world. It can be expected to worsen poverty, have a significant impact on global migration patterns, and risk tipping fragile states into instability, conflict and state failure.[15]

In announcing one of its reports, the Indian Energy and Resources Institute (TERI) said:

> population growth is often cited as a significant factor contributing to environmental degradation. What is not so discussed, however, is the impact that the degradation of the environment often has on population movements. There is no dispute over the impacts of population movements on the environment, especially where such movement contributes to urbanization. But, this movement may, in the first place, be triggered by environmental problems. The people who seek refuge from these environmental problems by moving to another destination are referred to as environmental refugees.[16]

Since climate change is set to affect Africa and Asia in particular it can be expected that population movements from these continents will increase in the coming decades; thus placing more pressure on Europe's southern and eastern boundaries. The declining domestic populations of EU countries coupled with a general rise in climate and economic migration may produce a new dynamic in the labour markets of the EU. Currently 85% of migrant labour in the EU is unskilled, with 5% classed as skilled.[17] A decline in the domestic labour forces may increase demand for migrant labour.

Climate change in Central and South Asia is likely to force people to move westward towards Europe. Among the risks posed by climate change to human security the International Panel on Climate Change (IPCC) has highlighted is the risk posed by glacial melt. Of direct relevance to Europe and the challenge of climate-induced migration is glacial melt in the Himalayas and other Asian mountain ranges which may first result in flooding and then water shortages which lead to crop failure and possible food shortages. The World Wildlife Fund (WWF) has reported that 67% of all Himalayan glaciers are retreating. Research has shown that glacial melt in the Ak-Shrak range in Central Asia accelerated after 1977.[18] Professor Stephan Harrison of Exeter University highlights the fact that glacial melt in the Tien Shan Mountains could lead to 'profound changes which may affect the livelihoods of millions of people in Central Asia'.[19] Initially flooding in this area may cause old Soviet-era reservoirs to overflow, which could displace populations. As the melt slows and water becomes scarce, particularly in Kyrgyzstan, Uzbekistan and Turkmenistan, migrant flows of predominantly agrarian communities are likely to increase towards the West. Harrison also highlights the need for investment in the Central Asian water systems to offset the consequences of glacial melt.

Europe's own changing climate may lead to internal migration northwards as the climate warms up and affects southern European countries. In the east of Europe population displacement may more likely be caused by flooding in large river systems such as the Danube. The diversity of possible climate related migrations into and within the European space has the potential to alter its demography in unforeseen ways.

The challenge of urbanisation

The issue of urbanisation is a major security challenge for societies around the world. According to the UN 95% of annual population growth today is in urban areas. In some cities this has given rise to the phenomenon of 'mega-cities' and 'mega-slums'. In Central and Latin America, Mexico City, São Paulo and Rio de Janeiro are three examples. Elsewhere, Lagos provides a good example of the scale of the problem: a population of 300,000 in 1950 has risen to 13m today. By 2050 it is estimated that Lagos will have a population of 25m. In mega-slums communities grow up on the fringes of societies. The infrastructure of the host cities cannot cope with the additional quantities of people who then construct their own societies, their own rule of law and their own employments which rely on illicit and non-state activities based on a Darwinian 'survival of the fittest' culture. This culture in its turn is based around and is 'governed' by armed gangs which interact with each other. For Europe, which is unlikely to spawn mega-slums of its own in the near future, the risk is in importing problems (principally crime) in the form of immigrants from the mega cities of Latin America, Africa, and Asia.

The upward trend in urbanisation in Europe is lower than in Africa, Asia or Latin America, but is nonetheless increasing. The proportion of European residents living in urban areas is rising from 51.2% in 1950 to an estimated 72.6% by 2010 and

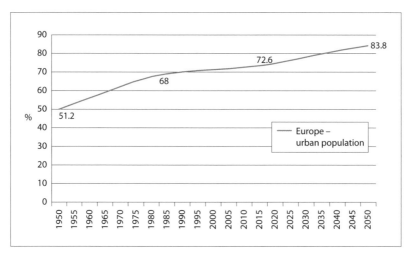

Figure 4: **% Annual growth trends in European urbanisation 1950–2050**[21]

over 80% by 2050.[20] At the same time it is predicted that overall population growth in Europe will slow between 2025 and 2050, at which point populations will start to decline overall as urbanisation increases. The increase in urbanisation moving ahead of overall population growth means that population densities will also increase, giving rise to security and health concerns. There is also an open question as to whether the pressure of growing urban populations as well as overall demographic growth in Asia and Africa will increase the pressure on people to migrate in greater numbers than are expected. Certainly, a possible reduction in the availability of water in those areas due to climate change is likely to increase this possibility.

Disease, migration and demography

The growing tide of migrants moving towards Europe from the South and East also presents an increasing risk of disease. The global trend towards urbanisation has led to the creation of mega-cities and mega-slums in developing countries. The density of population in these slum areas could mean that disease will spread faster. Migrants from these areas are therefore more likely to be 'carriers' of disease, raising the requirement for screening and possibly treatment and immunisation programmes in the countries of migrant origin. However, such measures will not be able to take account of the growing numbers of illegal immigrants, which underlines the requirement for tougher border controls throughout the European area and a health screening system for 'illegals' who are intercepted. This latter measure is to ensure that a migrant being returned to his or her country of origin has been screened as part of the process of gathering health data on migrant donor countries and to inform the country of origin for its own benefit.

The European Journal of Public Health reported in 2005 that 'International Migration challenges Tuberculosis (TB) control'.[22] The report highlighted the fact that since the mid-1990s the incidence of TB in the EU decreased to its lowest rate of 13.8 cases per 100,000 in 2005. However, 30% of cases were found in people of 'foreign origin (16% from Asia and Africa, and 8% from a non-EU country of Europe or of the former Soviet Union [FSU])'. The trend was for an increase in TB among immigrants and a decrease in the domestic population, emphasising the need for support for TB control in the migrants' countries of origin. The report concluded: 'Migration in Europe causes a shift in disease patterns. Migrant populations take their disease patterns to the new areas of residence … A vaccination policy should regard Europe as one population and target the infectious diseases at source.'

Apart from the threat of disease carried by immigrants, the rapid spread of A/H1N1 (swine flu) in 2009 and its designation as a Level 6 pandemic by the World Health Organisation (WHO) has demonstrated the danger of a rapid spread of disease as a result of a more globalised travel system. The trend in intercontinental travel as a matter of routine for tourists, business people and immigrants visiting relatives in their countries of

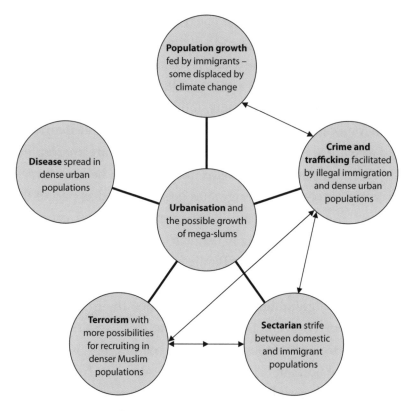

Figure 5: **Connectivity between population trends and threats to Europe**
(Source: Giegerich and Comolli, eds, 'FORESEC Deliverable D4.5 Report on European Security: Trends, Drivers, Threats', 2009, p. 61. http://foresec/eu/)

origin creates an ever-present risk of disease 'jumping' from one part of the world to another.

Summary of risks

In a world which has become globalised, the links between population growth, terrorism and emerging risks associated with climate change, urbanisation and disease are increasing.

Growing numbers of immigrants from Muslim countries implanted in domestic and indigenous European communities present greater recruiting opportunities for anti-Western jihadists. The differences in national policies governing the proscription of proselyte organisations, such as Hizb-ut-Tahrir, which espouse global Islamic agendas, are advantageous to jihadists. Therefore there may be an argument in favour of a coordinated policy to ensure that proscription in one country does not mean that either a group goes underground and adopts a more sinister agenda, or it moves to another country where it is not proscribed; thus creating a greater density of potential or actual militancy. The implicit risk in demographic terms is in the unintended consequences of un-coordinated and diverse policies within the EU area. Displacement because of fear of arrest or racist aggression simply moves the problem from one country to another, possibly causing imbalance in the ethnic make-up of the 'receiver' society.

The issue of population growth and crime in urban areas is another area of growing concern. If numbers of immigrants, many of whom are likely to be illegal, increase, tensions and competition are likely to rise unless infrastructures and policies are strengthened to ensure peaceful cohabitation among different groups. Policing and health care are two critical areas in the reduction of the human-security risks associated with urbanisation. The enforcement of the rule of law is more difficult in populated urban areas, due to increasing densities where gangs can emerge as the local arbiters in security if allowed to do so. In this scenario policing will become more expensive.

The major economic powers in Europe are tightening their immigration laws and procedures. However, the need for migrant labour in Europe is likely to increase as domestic population numbers fall. This dynamic will necessitate careful regulation as it may lead to internecine strife in some European countries, and particularly in dense conurbations such as Paris. While increased migration flows into EU countries would require substantial social and cultural adjustments, it is important to keep in mind that alternative policies to meet demographic challenges may also demand far-reaching changes.

The EU's response to the pressures of climate-induced immigration has yet to be tested. There is a danger that excessive measures to curb any influx, such as policies of exclusion affecting immigrants who have been forced to move by the affects of climate change, could run counter to Europe's humanitarian principles, leading to possible legal challenges or a change in those principles.

A greater density of population in urban areas carries a higher risk of disease. Health care budgets may come under pressure and as a preventive measure to stop the spread of disease leading to pandemics of the swine flu variety; health screening for legal immigrants may have to take place in their countries of origin. Migrants will increasingly come from dense conurbations and may therefore be more likely to be carriers of disease.

Responses and policy approaches

Domestic demographic challenges and pressures caused by current immigration policies increasingly affect the majority of EU and other European states. However, responses, rather than being transnational in character, are still based largely on national policies that react to the demands of domestic labour markets, post-colonial agreements and national security concerns, rather than recognising the transnational or even global nature of the problem. The 'Blue Card' scheme originally proposed as a mechanism to filter migration so that only highly skilled workers can enter the EU on time-limited work permits is one example. The scheme looks set to come into force with the UK, Ireland and Denmark choosing to opt out.

The labour demand caused by a declining domestic population results in a need for a fluctuating proportion of migrant workers to fill gaps in European workforces, but also creates the potential for instability and internal conflict. In 2009 the

EU introduced the Blue Card scheme to streamline the process for highly qualified immigrant workers, which has raised the question: does the scheme undermine the ability of developing nations to build their own capacity by attracting them to Europe? All five major EU economies (France, the UK, Germany, Spain and Italy) have tightened their laws and procedures governing immigration in recent years and introduced selective criteria. This chapter does not examine immigration policies in detail, except to highlight the present and possible future impacts that they may have on the demographic map of Europe and the human-security risks that they may carry. The location of Spain and Italy, on the southern perimeter of Europe, makes them cases in point: this is where immigration control is likely to be most tested by climate-induced migration from North Africa and the Sahel.

Spain is a destination for legal and illegal migrants from African countries as well as immigrants from the Spanish-speaking countries of Latin America. Until 2007, Spanish immigration policy was lenient towards immigrants as there were sufficient employment opportunities in Spain to meet the demands of the growing Spanish economy. However in 2009 with unemployment at 19% the government tightened the laws governing immigration and introduced an incentive scheme to induce unemployed immigrants to return to their countries of origin for at least three years. As an example of the scale of immigration which was driving economic growth, the Spanish National Institute of Statistics reported that between 1998 and 2009 the immigrant population of Spain grew from 2% to 11% of the total population.

Italy has reacted in a similar way to Spain by instituting strict laws to curb immigration. The 'Bossi–Fini' law of 2002, which imposed an annual quota on migrant workers allowed into Italy, has been replaced by legislation that requires foreign workers to be hired by employers before they leave their home countries. Italy also follows the EU-wide trend of offering preferred employment status to skilled and qualified migrant workers.

Demographic trends and drivers in Europe demand solutions that may not be attractive to national and traditionally minded policymakers. Domestic populations in some countries are falling, while immigration levels remain high. Across the EU, the Muslim birth rate is three times higher than the non-Muslim birth rate, putting the Muslim population on course to double to 20m by 2020, if current trends continue.[23] The global economic crisis has had the effect of slowing immigration in some states, but the reduction is mostly in migrants who move from one European country to another.

European states in general seem to be responding to the challenges posed by this juxtaposition of demographic challenges, by instituting policies based on the need to protect jobs for ageing populations. The pressure of migration towards, rather than within, Europe is likely to increase as climate change affects areas already beset by poor living standards to the south and east of Europe. The EU remains an attractive destination for people from underdeveloped and developing countries as well as for those involved in illicit trade and trafficking.

The challenge is how to stem the tide of immigration without compromising those human rights which have so long been championed by Europe. To refuse asylum to the oppressed may run counter to the principles of the EU. Yet this is a real possibility if human security within Europe is to be protected under existing national policies. In order to contribute to global peace and stability, the EU has a responsibility to offer protection to those in need of it and to address the root causes of forced migration. The migration debate should be kept distinct from the refugee debate, which is about protecting basic needs and upholding human-rights commitments. Arguably, in this developing context, a common pan-European approach, if not a strategy, must be pursued. Apart from climate-induced migrations on the borders of Europe, the growing threat of pandemics spreading quickly in a more urbanised continent has to be grasped. Immigration may feed into the risk of disease as more migrants from the mega-cities of Europe, Latin America and Asia arrive. While the security implications of migration are manifold, care has to be taken not to reduce migration to issues of hard security such as by the overuse of repressive counter-terrorism measures. The migration debate needs to be multi-dimensional.

CHAPTER FOUR

Terrorism in Europe

Nigel Inkster

Director of Transnational Threats and Political Risk, IISS

In the past, the methodology of terrorist groups active in Europe, such as ETA and the Provisional IRA (PIRA), has been characterised as 'a lot of people watching, not many dead';[1] in other words, attacks were designed to draw attention to a particular cause and to pressurise governments into negotiation, but not to inflict large numbers of casualties for their own sake. Al-Qaeda, on the other hand, has focused from the outset on mass-casualty attacks and on targets of economic significance. Its approach resembles conventional warfare, with the effect being enhanced by the widespread use of suicide bombers. Moreover, in contrast to groups such as PIRA, it is not clear what kind of political accommodation could realistically be reached with al-Qaeda, even assuming that European governments might be prepared to contemplate such an option. Europe has also experienced a degree of international terrorism, from groups such as the Palestinian Black September and others linked to the Iranian, Libyan and Syrian states having undertaken a variety of attacks in France, Germany, Greece and the UK. This latter phenomenon has not been evident for some years, though there is justifiable concern that if the current Iranian regime perceives itself to be under pressure from European states over its nuclear programme, it may retaliate with terrorist attacks conducted by the paramilitary Iranian Revolutionary Guard–Quds Force and its proxies.

Transnational Islamist terrorism in Europe

The new element in the equation has been transnational terrorism, a phenomenon which began to manifest itself only after the turn of the millennium, but whose roots significantly predate that period. Europe has seen a substantial growth in its resident Islamic populations since the 1950s. The first wave of Muslim immigration into Europe took place in the 1950s and 1960s. In the case of the UK, the overwhelming majority of Muslim immigrants came from Pakistani Azad Kashmir. During the same period, Germany began to import large numbers of Turkish *Gastarbeiter*, or guest workers, to assist in post-war economic reconstruction, while in France the legacy of colonial wars resulted in large numbers of Algerian immigrants resettling. In all three cases, these communities established themselves at the margins of European society and had little incentive – or indeed encouragement – to integrate into the mainstream. This was not seen as a security problem other than in terms of its potential to generate periodic racial tensions. During the 1970s and early 1980s, this first wave of immigrants was supplemented by an influx from a wider range of Islamic states, most of which were accepted by Northern European states such as Denmark, the Netherlands and Sweden on humanitarian grounds. This second wave found themselves in some respects more marginalised than the first as they lacked marketable skills and generally found themselves living on welfare. The third wave came in the 1990s, when substantial numbers of Algerians sought refuge in a number of European countries following the 1992 military coup and the subsequent upsurge in terrorist violence. Many of them saw Europe as only a temporary refuge pending a resolution of events within their own country.

The politicisation of Europe's Islamic communities arguably began in the mid-1980s when the Arab-language media moved en masse from Beirut to London as a consequence of the Lebanese civil war. London became the opinion-forming centre of the Islamic world and also a proxy battleground for a range of competing interest groups within it. This concentration of intellectual and opinion-forming activity, together with the UK's status as a global communications and financial centre and the development of an increasingly multicultural society, made the UK an attractive destination for thinkers and activists unable to operate in their countries of origin. Among Middle Eastern communities established in London in the 1980s and 1990s were many from Arab opposition movements, including the Egyptian and Syrian Muslim Brotherhoods and Saudi opposition groups such as Sa'ad al Faqih's Movement for Islamic Reform in Arabia. Also represented were Algerian opposition groups – already well established in France and to a lesser degree Spain – and the anti-Gadhafi Libyan Islamic Fighting Group. This concentration of activity, which the British government sought to monitor, but not to hinder, led increasingly frustrated foreign governments including Algeria, France and Saudi Arabia, who were the target of much of this activity, to refer to the UK capital as Londonistan.

The other key ingredient in the radicalisation of Europe's Islamic communities was the development of a culture of jihadism which grew out of the war of resistance in Afghanistan against the Soviet Union. The end of the anti-Soviet jihad saw significant numbers of veteran fighters disperse back to their countries of origin, including within Europe, from where many moved back and forth to other conflicts such as Bosnia,

Chechnya and Afghanistan once the Taliban regime became established there in 1996. Around the same time, the al-Qaeda brand of extremism was beginning to be promoted by radical preachers such as Abu Qatada, Abu Hamza al Masri and Omar Bakri Mohamed, the founder of al-Muhajiroun, a UK-based proselytising movement, many of whose adherents subsequently graduated to terrorist activities. The al-Qaeda message, which exploited the emergence of the Internet to propagate itself, resonated particularly with second- and third-generation European Muslims suffering from issues of identity and also of frustrated expectations. It was the coming together of all these elements that led to the phenomenon of home-grown Islamist terrorism within the European Union, as individuals and groups primarily involved in support activities for terrorist groups slowly began to refocus their attention on Europe as a terrorist target. This process predated both the invasion of Afghanistan in 2001 and the invasion of Iraq, though both these events undoubtedly acted as catalysts for the radicalisation process.

The earliest manifestation of this jihadism occurred in France, beginning with an unsuccessful attempt in 1994 to hijack an airliner and fly it into the Eiffel Tower, a bombing campaign in 1995 which led to eight deaths and 150 injuries and an unsuccessful attempt to commit atrocities during the 1998 football World Cup. These attacks were undertaken by Algerian jihadists who had fought with the 'Afghan Arabs' in the anti-Soviet jihad and had then joined the Armed Islamic Group of Algeria (GIA)'s terrorism campaign against the Algerian military government. Foot soldiers were recruited from within France's Algerian diaspora community. There have been no successful attacks in France since 1995 but the French security authorities have foiled numerous attempts since that date and the threat continues to be seen as real. In the main, terrorist plots in France appear to be indigenously developed with no strong evidence of outside involvement. There has been an expectation that ever since the Algerian terrorists the Salafist Group for Preaching and Combat (GSPC) reinvented itself as al-Qaeda in the Islamic Maghreb (AQIM), swearing an oath of allegiance to Osama bin Ladin in 2006, it would seek to inspire attacks in France. Until recently, there has been no evidence of this with AQIM activities in France apparently restricted to revenue-raising and logistic activities in support of efforts to send militants from the Maghreb to take part in jihad in Iraq and, latterly, Afghanistan. But since 2007 some 30 European citizens have been kidnapped or killed by AQIM in the Sahel region, the most recent case involving seven employees of the French nuclear company Areva in northern Niger in September 2010.

From France, the phenomenon of Islamist terrorism has spread to most countries in Western Europe, with the risk particularly salient for those countries supporting US-led coalition activities in Iraq and Afghanistan, though to date the new accession states of Eastern Europe have been largely immune from the problem. The number of successful terrorist attacks within Europe has been relatively small; the French bombings in 1995, the Madrid bombings and the murder of Dutch film-maker Theo van Gogh in 2004 and the London bombings in 2005. But this relatively small number of incidents belies the scale of the threat, which is better illustrated by the substantially greater number of plots that have been thwarted and the number of individuals who have been arrested and convicted of terrorist offences or who are under observation by European security services and police forces.

A particular problem is the continuing appeal exercised by al-Qaeda propaganda to young European Muslims. In the early days, the al-Qaeda message was conveyed by charismatic preachers such as Abu Hamza al Masri and by groups such as

Hizb-ut-Tahrir in obviously Islamic locations such as mosques and bookshops. But as the authorities have come to grips with these individuals and shut down extreme organisations, much of the radicalisation process now takes place on the Internet or among peer groups in more social settings. Noone can say with any confidence how many young European Muslims have been radicalised to the point of being willing to resort to violence: that depends on a range of factors, but many thousands will have been affected to some degree. Many are involved more in facilitation work such as raising money or providing for logistic support for young Muslims to take part in jihad in Iraq or Afghanistan. Experience has however shown that it is difficult to identify the point at which groups and individuals might make the transition from involvement in support activities to participation in attack planning.

Transnational terrorism, as practised by al-Qaeda and affiliated groups, has been characterised as a reaction by parts of the Islamic world to globalisation – accelerated by the collapse of the Soviet Union – which it perceived as tantamount to Westernisation.[2] Al-Qaeda's ideology derives from the ideology of the Muslim Brotherhood (Ikhwan al Muslimeen) as developed by Sayid Qutb; it is a combination of a particular fundamentalist interpretation of Islam and Leninist principles of political organisation. The ultimate targets of groups like al-Qaeda are not Western states but rather the so-called apostate regimes of the Islamic world which are seen as unjust, oppressive and un-Islamic. But these regimes – the Near Enemy – are seen as being dependent on the support of the US and other Western states – the Far Enemy. The strategy of al-Qaeda, since the mid-1990s, has been to focus attacks on the Far Enemy, in particular the US, with the aim of forcing it to abandon its activities in the Islamic world. Before the 2001 US-led invasion of Afghanistan, Europe was seen by al-Qaeda primarily as a safe base, although the first known terrorist attempt by an al-Qaeda-related individual took place in 2000 in the UK.[3] But since the invasion of Afghanistan, and the subsequent invasion of Iraq, states seen as close US allies have found themselves increasingly subject to attack.

This new strain of terrorism differs in some key attributes from anything that has gone before. Al-Qaeda is as much an ideological movement as a terrorist organisation, and is able to attach itself to a multiplicity of grievances. It is not defined by geography and is capable of manifesting itself in many different locations. Attacks may be undertaken by groups located in specific European countries but operational planning and training will often be conducted outside Europe. Many young European Muslims have gone to Afghanistan, Iraq and Somalia to engage in jihad. No official statistics exist but one source has spoken of 4,000 British nationals undergoing such training.[4] A separate source talks of 'hundreds' of German residents, mostly of ethnic Turkish origin undertaking jihad in Afghanistan and Pakistan.[5] Some have been turned around and sent back to Europe to undertake terrorist acts. At the same time, attacks against the US and other states have been undertaken by groups based predominantly in Europe. This process began with the 9/11 attack whose ringleaders Mohamed Atta, Marwan al Shehhi, Ziad Jarrah and Ramzi Binalshibh had all worshipped at the Al Quds mosque in Hamburg before moving – albeit without Binalshibh, who was unable to obtain a visa – to the US to undertake pre-attack flight training. (The Al Quds mosque, since reopened as the Taiba mosque, appears to remain a centre of jihadism. Ahmed Siddiqi, a German resident of Afghan origin who was arrested in Afghanistan in July 2010 in connection with an al-Qaeda plan to undertake fedayeen attacks in Germany, France and the UK, had been a worshipper there.)[6]

The history of counter-terrorism efforts within Europe since 2000 has been one of adaptation to a new form of terrorism that has challenged traditional perceptions and capabilities, while in some cases continuing to manage more traditional threats. This has posed some difficult questions of political, judicial, administrative and social systems that had not been configured to deal with a transnational challenge of this kind. Consequently, European states have had to undertake a radical revision of concepts of national security. Europe has also not been immune from the impact of a globally structured US response to the phenomenon of al-Qaeda, conceived in terms of a 'war on terror'. This approach, which involved the use of a range of techniques incompatible with European norms and values, has generated significant controversy and trans-Atlantic political tension. Since coming to office in 2008, President Barack Obama has repudiated the use of so-called 'enhanced interrogation' techniques and has closed the so-called black (i.e., undeclared) detention centres run by the CIA, but rendition continues, Guantanamo Bay remains open despite efforts by the Obama administration to close it, and debate continues about whether to try some terrorist suspects in military tribunals. Moreover, the Obama administration has maintained a heightened tempo of drone attacks against al-Qaeda in Pakistan (rising from 53 in 2009 to 85 by the third quarter of 2010[7]), an approach which many in Europe find legally, ethically and strategically questionable. Despite some approximation, Europe and the US continue to see terrorism in very different terms. Efforts to reconcile these differences through a commonly agreed Set of Principles appear for the moment to be stalled.

European ethno-separatist and other terrorist groups

Terrorism has been a feature of Europe's political landscape for almost as long as the concept of the modern nation-state has existed. Terrorist movements in Europe could, until the recent advent of transnational terror, be divided into two broad categories: ethno-separatist, such as the Irish Republican Army (IRA), Basque separatists ETA and Corsican separatists (FLNC-UC); and ideological, such as the Red Brigades, Red Army Faction and November 17. There is, however, more than an element of overlap between these two strains: PIRA and ETA, for example, have espoused an ill-defined socialist ideology, while neo-Nazi groups, whose use of violence has so far been restricted to sporadic attacks on ethnic minority groups and individuals, combine an extreme right-wing ideology with a focus on ethnic and racial purity. European terrorist groups have largely confined their activities to attacks on targets within national boundaries while seeking political support, finance and weaponry from overseas.

Northern Ireland

Despite the PIRA ceasefire in 1994 and the signing of the Good Friday Agreement in 1998, sectarian tensions remain a very real threat to the peace in Northern Ireland. The Good Friday Agreement began a process of decommissioning and reintegration into civil society of the bulk of the PIRA. It also brought the leaders of Sinn Féin, the political wing of the Republican Movement, into mainstream politics, in a difficult but apparently durable power-sharing arrangement with Loyalist politicians. The political process has been helped by the decision of the two main Loyalist paramilitary groups, the Ulster Volunteer Force (UVF) and the Ulster Defence Association (UDA), to decommission their weapons. But the Republican movement has not forsaken its ultimate objective of a united Ireland: three Republican extremist groups, the Real IRA (RIRA), the Continuity IRA (CIRA) and Oglaigh na hEirreann, have refused to renounce violence and sought to exploit persisting tensions, mounting terrorist attacks in Northern Ireland, the Republic of Ireland and mainland UK. These organisations remain relatively weak, extensively penetrated by the UK and Irish security forces and lacking in widespread appeal. They also lack the levels of US political and financial support enjoyed by the PIRA from its founding at the beginning of the troubles in 1969 until the signing of the Good Friday Agreement. But even in their current, debilitated state the dissidents retain the capacity to have significant effect, as shown by the March 2009 attack on the Massereene Barracks in Northern Ireland, which resulted in the deaths of two British soldiers. Violence during the summer 2010 marching season also appeared to suggest that ten years of relative stability in Northern Island may be under threat from dissident Republicans. The results of a poll undertaken by the University of Liverpool and released on 5 October 2010 shows that 14% of Republicans 'have sympathy for the reasons' why RIRA and CIRA continue to engage in violence with levels of support especially prevalent among young males.[8] In the event that sectarian tensions in Northern Ireland boil over, or the political process comes under strain, this appeal could further increase, and significant resources would be tied up in monitoring these groups for as long as they are considered a threat. The UK Security Service has been obliged to open a substantial office in Northern Ireland to assume responsibilities that had previously belonged to the Royal Ulster Constabulary Special Branch – whose disbandment has led to a significant loss of knowledge and expertise at a time when security services are fully stretched dealing with the Islamist terrorist threat.

Spain

A process of devolution more extensive than any other within the EU has failed to neutralise a hard core of Basque activists, who remain committed to the creation of an independent Basque state encompassing the three Basque provinces, Navarre in Spain, and the Basque regions of France. The principal Basque terrorist group ETA (Euskadi ta Askatasuna) has pursued this objective through a campaign of bombings, assassinations, kidnappings, intimidation and extortion. Periodic efforts by the Spanish government to reach a political settlement with ETA and its now-banned political wing Herri Batasuna – the most recent initiated by Prime Minister José Luis Zapatero in 2006 – have foundered in the face of intransigence. This appears to originate from a group of young activists, many of whom graduated from the organised street violence (*kale borroka*) which forms an integral part of ETA tactics within the Basque region. Enhanced coordination between the security authorities of Spain and France has largely denied ETA activists the French safe havens they had previously enjoyed and has led to the detention of successive iterations of the ETA leadership and the seizure of large quantities of weapons. Efforts by ETA to use Portugal as an operating base have also been largely frustrated. Apparently as a result of the sustained security pressure to which they had been subjected, the leadership of ETA announced a ceasefire on 5 September 2010, which they characterised three weeks later as 'permanent and verifiable'. The Spanish government has, however, rejected this initiative as insufficient, citing the fact that ETA has a long track record of unilaterally breaking ceasefires. It demanded that the organisation commit permanently to abandoning violence before any political negotiations can be entertained. The reservations of the Spanish government are probably well founded. It is far from certain that the current leadership of ETA has the capacity to hold the organisation together and to enter into a credible political negotiation; and it is likely that those elements who continue to favour violence will at some point seek to reassert themselves.

Greece

Two anarcho-syndicalist groups, Epanastatikos Agonas (Revolutionary Struggle) and Sehta Epanastaton (Sect of Revolutionaries), emerged as part of a recent resurgence of anarchism in Greek society. This culminated in widespread public disorder in parts of Athens in early 2009 and again in May 2010, in response to the government's introduction of austerity measures. But public revulsion following the deaths of three bank workers in a fire started by anarchist protesters has compelled these groups to adopt a much lower profile. Attacks undertaken by Epanastatikos Agonas have been mainly random, unprofessional and not notably successful. In March 2010, following a police shootout with a suspected member of Epanastatikos Agonas, the Greek security police arrested six members of the group whom they had under surveillance, in the process finding a range of weaponry, explosives and attack plans. Although it was initially thought that these arrests had effectively brought this problem to an end, the explosion of a parcel bomb in the office of Greek Minister for Public Order Michalis Chrysochoidis in June 2010, which killed the head of his security detail, suggested that Epanastatikos Agonas has retained some capacity to do damage.

Greece's other main anarcho-syndicalist terrorist group, Sehta Epanastaton, has engaged in targeted killing, showing evidence of forethought and planning more typical of Greece's earliest anarcho-syndicalist groups, Epanastatikos Laikos Agonas (ELA) and November 17 (N17), which formed in the 1970s after the restoration of democracy in the country. Sehta Epanastaton's recent activities include the murder in early 2009 of an officer of the security police, who was providing protection for a witness who had previously testified against members of ELA, and the murder in July 2010 of investigative journalist Sokrates Giolas.

As was the case with the now-defunct N17, Sehta Epanastaton and Epanastatikos Agonas are small and tightly knit, making it hard for the security forces to penetrate them. A wider problem in dealing with these groups is that there still exists among many Greek politicians and opinion-formers a degree of tolerance of anarchism, which translates into a lack of political will to address the problem of domestic terrorism. Efforts are, however, now under way to introduce legislation to strengthen the investigative and intelligence gathering capabilities of the Greek Anti-Terrorist Police (DAEV). Its technical capabilities have been enhanced and a more collaborative culture introduced into Greece's wider security community. But the Anti-Terrorist Police still suffer from low levels of public co-operation and inadequate resources and skills, and it remains uncertain whether they will be able to tackle the problem that has been a feature of Greek society since the 1960s, when anarchists formed a significant component of the political resistance to the military junta. At that time, N17 and ELA carried out targeted assassinations, bank robberies and a large number of lesser attacks on property. Their leaders are now imprisoned.

Evidence has recently emerged of terrorist activities by anarchist groups in Italy, consisting mainly of sending parcel bombs to members of the Carabinieri, apparently in retribution for activities undertaken by the Greek security authorities against Sehta Epanastaton. It is currently unclear whether this activity consists of spontaneous acts by ideologically aligned groups or whether, as some members of the Greek security services suspect, these activities have been deliberately orchestrated by Sehta and related Greek groups.

Red Brigades

Since 2003, there have been no attacks attributed to the Red Brigades. Six members were arrested by the Italian police in

2003 and in 2005 another four were imprisoned for murder. The Red Brigades were founded in 1970 and throughout the ensuing decade presented a substantial threat to the security of the state. Their most spectacular coups were the kidnapping and murder of politician Aldo Moro in 1978 and the kidnapping of US Brigadier-General James Dozier in 1981, but they were also responsible for numerous attacks against police, lawyers, politicians and other manifestations of state authority. By the early 1980s the Red Brigades had been largely dismantled but around the turn of the millennium a number of targeted assassinations raised fears that the group may have become reactivated.

Neo-Nazis

Most European countries have some kind of neo-Nazi group, though in most cases these operate on the fringes of conventional politics with violence limited to random attacks on individual immigrants or immigrant communities. It is hard to assess the overall impact of such groups, especially in countries such as Germany and Austria, where the degree of attention they receive from the security authorities tends to result in an overly alarmist depiction of the seriousness of the threat. However, in the UK, in June 2008 Martyn Gilleard was sentenced to 11 years' imprisonment for terrorist offences. Gilleard, who was acting alone, had amassed four nail bombs and a collection of blade weapons. His declared objective was 'to save Britain from multi-racial peril'.[9] In July 2009, London's Metropolitan Police revealed details of an investigation into a right-wing extremist group in possession of rocket launchers and pipe bombs with apparent links to similar groups in Europe, Australia and New Zealand.[10] And the murder in the US on 10 June 2009 of a security guard at the Holocaust Museum is another poten-tially worrying concern, not least because the perpetrator was a member of the Friends of the British National Party, an entity set up in the US to raise funds for this right-wing party. Right-wing, anti-immigration groups appear to be a growing phenomenon in Eastern European states such as the Czech Republic and Hungary, but to date such groups have restricted themselves to organised rallies and the dissemination of anti-immigration propaganda.

Strategy and tactics

A key issue which has preoccupied security and intelligence officers in European countries is the degree to which Islamist terrorist activity in Europe is the work of small, disaggregated groups inspired by the al-Qaeda ideology and to what extent such activities are the product of external direction by the al-Qaeda leadership. Between the US invasion of Afghanistan in 2001 and 2004, any activity undertaken in Europe was probably the result of individual initiative. But by 2004, the al-Qaeda leadership had re-established itself in the Federally Administered Tribal Areas of Pakistan (FATA) to the point where it was in a position to focus on attack planning in Europe. This first became evident in the UK, where a large Pakistani diaspora provided the mechanism whereby al-Qaeda was able to make contact with and mobilise radicalised young British Muslims, many of whom travelled to Pakistan to take part in jihadist training, largely with a view to fighting the US-led coalition in Afghanistan. Once in the training camps, some of the more promising students were recruited to undertake terrorist acts in the UK. Most of the terrorist investigations within the UK which have resulted in arrests and convictions, as well as the 7 July 2005 suicide bombings and the attempted bombings two weeks later, were the product of this process and showed clear signs of external planning and direction.

This phenomenon has been repeated in both Denmark, where the security service (PET) disrupted a number of plots directed from Pakistan, in Norway and in Germany. There the bulk of the problem is to be found within Germany's large Turkish diaspora, which has been targeted by the Islamic Jihad Union, a Pakistan-based Uzbekh group closely allied with al-Qaeda, which runs jihadi training camps and has attempted to radicalise Turkish communities in Western Europe with substantial quantities of online Turkish-language propaganda. A final example is Spain, which in 2008 witnessed attempts to infiltrate the country by a Pakistani cell apparently directed by then Pakistani Taliban leader Baitullah Mesud.

Over the course of 2010 there have been signs pointing to a greater dispersal and diversification of jihadist terrorism. Pakistan remains the headquarters of al-Qaeda's leadership and the most serious attack plotting continues to emanate from the country. Although al-Qaeda remains under significant pressure from CIA drone attacks, its level of ambition is undiminished and indeed arguably enhanced. Al-Qaeda is increasingly working through like-minded groups such as the Haqqani network, a Pakistan-based jihadist group operating in Afghanistan, and other indigenous Pakistani extremist groups such as Lashkar-e-Taiba which, though focused primarily on India, has developed transnational networks which it has proven willing to share with al-Qaeda.

Transnational attacks have now begun to emanate from Yemen, where al-Qaeda in the Arabian Peninsula has experienced a revival. There are fears that the same may be true in respect of al-Qaeda in the Islamic Maghreb. There is also evidence groups are adapting their techniques in response to the operations under way against them. For example, Anwar al Awlaki, the US–Yemeni dual national ideologue now located in Yemen, has told aspiring jihadis that it is no longer necessary to focus on planning spectacular mass-casualty attacks against high-profile targets and that efforts should be made to undertake whatever attacks appear feasible. The US has already witnessed a range of al-Qaeda-inspired attacks, including the shooting in 2009 of two US Army recruiters by a young convert to Islam and mass-shootings such as that carried out at Fort Hood army base in Texas the same year. In late September 2010 details emerged of a plot by the Haqqani network, working in conjunction with al-Qaeda, to undertake coordinated fedayeen attacks – similar to those which took place in Mumbai in 2008 – in France, Germany and the UK. While ethnicity has never been a defining character-istic of al-Qaeda cells, there is also some evidence of increasing ethnic diversity among jihadis. A terrorist cell detained in Oslo, Norway, in July 2010 was made up of a Uighur, an Uzbekh and an Iraqi Kurd. And there are more converts starting to feature in jihadist plots, as evidenced by two of the men convicted of the 2007 Sauerland plot in Germany, which involved planned bombings of Ramstein air base and Frankfurt airport.

The fact that for five years no successful jihadist terror-ist attacks have taken place in Europe should thus offer no grounds for complacency. Even if al-Qaeda has failed in its aim of bringing about a revolution in the Islamic world, its 'brand' and ideology continue to hold a powerful attraction for vulner-able young Muslims who may have a pre-existing grievance. Al-Qaeda had developed a corpus of jihadist theology which has proven robust and resilient even in the face of public recan-tations by some of its authors. There is moreover no shortage of perceived grievances to which the al-Qaeda ideology can attach itself, including the continuing conflict in Afghanistan and the unresolved questions of Palestine and Kashmir. Further attacks can be expected along a spectrum of activity, ranging from acts by self-radicalised individuals acting unsupported to more organised attacks by home-grown groups with little external direction or even major attacks conceived and directed from outside Europe. The impact of such attacks may be lower than those previously attempted, but the frequency could be greater. There is no comfort to be taken from the prediction that attackers may act with little international support: the less organised the attackers, the harder they will prove to identify and deter.

Another key problem, which has not been successfully addressed, is that of convicted terrorists currently serving custodial sentences. Reliable figures are impossible to obtain, but it is clear that few if any of those who have been imprisoned for terrorist offences are repentant and many have actively exploited their status and reputation to recruit among prison populations which are by definition vulnerable. A report by the London-based counter-radicalisation think tank the Quilliam Foundation published in November 2009 has detailed the ways in which some of the estimated 100 inmates of British high-security prisons – Belmarsh, Long Lartin, Frankland, Woodhill and Whitemoor – who have been convicted of terrorist offences have developed networks of supporters and engaged in proselytising activities. Extremist ideologues such as Abu Qatada and Abu Hamza have allegedly been able to preach sermons and to smuggle out propaganda despite being subject to strict security regimes.[11]

A related and largely unrealised concern is that of 'blowback': the return to Europe of jihadis who have participated in recent conflicts such as Iraq, Afghanistan and Somalia. In respect of Iraq, this concern has proved to be misplaced. The only foreign fighters al-Qaeda in Mesopotamia (AQM) were interested in employing were those willing to become suicide bombers. So far there is little evidence that European jihadists from Afghanistan and Somalia have made their way back to Europe and the balance of probabilities is that most will be killed in situ.

Even if the threat of terrorism within Europe recedes, within a globalised world the threat of terrorism emanating from Europe is arguably as much a concern for security authorities. That is likely to be a more enduring problem and one that will be more difficult to deal with as the lines between clear-cut examples of terrorism and what might be presented as legitimate support for political causes outside the EU become blurred. The experiences of the UK in the 1990s and Germany since 2001 indicate that it is no longer realistic to tolerate activity that does not appear directly to threaten narrowly defined national security interests. Proselytising movements such as Hizb-ut-Tahrir and Tablighi Jemaat, both quintessentially transnational organisations, purport not to espouse violence. But their propagation of an extreme interpretation of Islam, their rejection of democracy as incompatible with Islamic values and their aspirations to replace what they perceive as apostate regimes in the Islamic world by avowedly extra-constitutional means raise some serious difficulties for security authorities and policymakers. Such organisations have served as a conveyor belt, bringing young Muslims close to the point where they risk slipping over into engagement in violence. These organisations are banned in some EU states but not in others. In countries where they are banned, as in the case of the UK-based al-Muhajiroun group, they tend to re-emerge under other identities but with an identical agenda.

A further complicating factor is that the issue of al-Qaeda-inspired terrorism is inextricably bound up with community relations, integration and tolerance. In some EU states, notably the UK, significant efforts have been made to address this problem, with a focus on efforts to promote an alternative to the al-Qaeda narrative and to secure the support of Islamic communities in identifying and rooting out extremist groups.[12] This approach is based on the perception that the magnitude of the problem of radicalised Islamic youth in the UK cannot be resolved simply by resorting to arrests and prosecutions. It has been difficult to implement, with objective criteria for measuring performance proving especially elusive. It has also raised questions over whether an exclusive focus on the problems posed by one community could in fact prove counter-productive, enhancing a sense of resentment and victimhood on the part of Islamic communities while simultaneously generating resentment within other communities who felt their concerns were going unaddressed. Many EU states have to some degree followed the UK model of the Contest counter-terrorism strategy, with its four strands: Protect, Prepare, Pursue and Prevent (with Prevent covering community relations and counter-radicalisation). But at the other end of the spectrum, France has consciously eschewed this approach, emphasising instead a policy of integration and *laïcité* (secularisation).

The European response

When the threat of Islamist terrorism first became evident within the EU, the technical capacity and the political will to respond varied considerably between states. France, with a long tradition of political policing, and with no other serious terrorist threats to confront, found itself well placed to react. Having initially failed to recognise the gravity of its internal security threat, the UK has deployed significant resources to deal with its problem. Overall, however, EU states have suffered from significant disparities in counter-terrorism capabilities. Many states lack the manpower, technical capacity, background knowledge and legislative authority to deal effectively with the threat. Examples include the reluctance of some states to permit eavesdropping operations and physical surveillance for intelligence-gathering rather than evidential purposes and the reluctance of others to insist on the retention of communications data. Building a 'common tool-kit' of measures for dealing with terrorism in a consistent manner will take time and some important discrepancies remain. To identify specific terrorist plots, Europe remains heavily dependent on US intelligence leads, generally derived from communications intercepts but sometimes as the result of prisoner interrogations. This arguably represents a vulnerability, which is not just operational but also political in cases where interrogations may have been accompanied by mistreatment or human-rights violations. These concerns can only be addressed by European governments exercising the political will to invest substantially in the kind of intelligence capacities they have, with one or two notable exceptions, been reluctant to do.

In 2005 the European Union launched its own Counter-Terrorism Strategy, similar in concept to the UK's Contest strategy, highlighting the Union's commitment 'to combat terrorism globally while respecting human rights, and make Europe safer, allowing its citizens to live in an area of freedom, security and justice'.[13] While acknowledging member states' main responsibility for combating terrorism, it aims to add value to national efforts by strengthening national capabilities, facilitating cooperation at the EU level, developing EU collective capabilities and promoting international partnerships outside the EU with the United Nations, NATO, the African Union and other international bodies and nations.

A number of proposals under review include the establishment of a Critical Infrastructure Warning Information Network and a European asylum support office. However, progress in some areas has been slow. In particular, technical limitations have prevented the implementation of the second generation of the Schengen Information System (SIS II), forcing the deadline to be pushed back to at least 2011. Also, strict data-protection rules are posing a barrier to the development of Europol's

Check the Web initiative. Cooperation among national agencies has increased not just between internal and external intelligence agencies and law enforcement but also between security agencies and other departments of central and local government responsible for such areas as community relations and education. And there appears to be willingness to export successful measures – such as in the case of local counter-radicalisation initiatives – to other member states. Yet at present it is hard to quantify success and it will take months or years to see whether EU measures are having a significant impact on countering the terrorist threat in Europe.

Conclusions

Counter-terrorism in Europe remains a national competence, reflecting the degree to which issues involving intelligence and security constitute one of the supreme expressions of national sovereignty. At a working level, operational cooperation between Europe's security and intelligence services has been good, with well-established mechanisms for information-sharing dating back to the 1970s. And the severity of the threat from transnational terrorism has impelled Europe's security and intelligence services to move from a Cold War-based need-to-know culture towards a need-to-share approach. There have been periodic suggestions that the EU should move towards establishing some kind of EU-wide counter-terrorism agency or that intelligence on terrorist suspects should be the subject of mandatory sharing. Such proposals are unlikely to prosper. Security and intelligence agencies constantly have to balance the need to use the intelligence they collect with the need to protect the sources of such intelligence. The originating service will thus always wish to be consulted about the use to which any piece of intelligence might be put, as only they can assess properly the consequent risk to the source – a concept referred to as the control principle. Moreover, countries such as the UK and France, which have invested heavily in security and intelligence capabilities, are likely to regard mandatory intelligence pooling initiatives or the creation of supra-national intelligence structures with suspicion, fearing that these represent an attempt by states not willing to make such investments to enjoy a free ride. Ultimately, there can be no way to compel states to share their information, nor to verify whether they have done so.

There is, however, an important role for the European Commission and other EU organs in creating an enabling environment for the effective conduct of counter-terrorism activities at a national level. Most recently, an initiative by EU states and the US to attempt to develop a common set of values to underpin joint counter-terrorism efforts, though slow to make progress, represents an important effort to mitigate the legal and ethical risks to which EU states have been exposed in earlier collaboration with the US. Much has already been done in terms of coordination and the provision of normative guidance in such areas as the development of common capabilities – the 'common tool-kit' – and in developing common approaches towards issues such as terrorist financing.

CHAPTER FIVE

Critical Infrastructure

Robert Whalley
Consulting Senior Fellow, International Institute for Strategic Studies

Introduction

Europe provides its citizens with relative prosperity, comfort and order in a crowded and fragile world. The territory of the European Union is a relatively small part of the total global surface. But it supports upwards of 500 million people who enjoy a comparatively secure and prosperous existence, built upon advanced social and political structures, economic development and extensive social capital and physical infrastructure. European countries are far from invulnerable to security threats, however: damage to the critical infrastructure could seriously challenge the European way of life. The spill of toxic sludge in Hungary in 2010, which at one point raised fears of pollution to the Danube, is a good example. There is considerable resilience and the capacity to mitigate potential damage built into the EU, within member states and in their constituent entities, in public and private corporations and in individual action. Recent mass-casualty terrorist attacks, environmental disasters and the global financial crisis have prompted the questions: how prepared is the EU for worst-case scenarios? How powerful will its response be in protecting critical infrastructures on which so many millions rely? There is much room for improvement in terms of making progress within its own space and institutions, but also in identifying those areas where Europe's influence is limited to that of a minor player on a global stage.

Concepts and definitions

The concept of a critical infrastructure does not lend itself to a ready definition. For many of the 500m or so citizens of the European Union, it may simply have no resonance at all, since it belongs to a world of authority or industrial or commercial organisation that rarely impinges on their lives, or only does so when things go radically wrong. It probably means much less to rural communities, which have well-developed traditions of self-help with minimal reliance on the state or on big institutions, compared to urban communities, whose active functioning is totally dependent on an integrated economic and physical environment, underpinned by a range of services designed to meet ever more advanced and sophisticated expectations.

For national, state and regional governments and governing elites, current thinking reflects recent history, and in particular the Cold War. For Western European countries, the issue was largely confined to a narrow list of military and national assets which might be thought vulnerable to armed attack or in armed conflict. A NATO rulebook would have included military and economic installations defined by their vulnerability to attack rather than by their political or economic significance. The probability of a power plant being taken out in the first wave of a Soviet *Spetsnaz* attack featured strongly in the tactical planning of national governments and their military, police and civil-defence capabilities.

The end of the Cold War made planning of this kind redundant, and in the relatively benign atmosphere after 1989 the urge to cash in a peace dividend has made it more difficult to maintain or develop further a modern concept of critical infrastructure. Certainly there was no rush to replace the old list with a new range of assets whose protection was an inescapable commitment of government.

Effects of economic liberalisation

A further complication was the drive to privatise public utilities, either as part of economic liberalisation in Western European countries or to encourage the injection of desperately needed capital into the economies of Eastern European countries, most of whom have joined the EU since the fall of the Berlin Wall. Individual initiative, deregulation and personal enterprise have provided the drivers for economic growth, leaving less room for government involvement or direction.

Furthermore, the rapid advance of pan-European economic enterprises, let alone those whose final ownership leads back to the United States, India, China or Russia, has made it increasingly difficult for governments to impose their requirements. Each such requirement has to be justified on its merits and in the face of legitimate commercial pressures to 'do the minimum'. It is one thing for governments to retain a 'golden share' when privatising a hitherto state-owned utility, quite another to enforce it in detail in the face of some unforeseen crisis such as a major environmental or climatic disaster, at a time when assets are strained and services are under pressure.

Progress in responding to challenges to critical infrastructure

The range of challenges

Just how far-reaching modern disasters can be was shown explicitly by the toxic spillage of chemical effluent from the Sandoz plant in Switzerland into the River Rhine in 1986, imperilling that mighty river as a source of water, transport, leisure facilities and much more, irrespective of national boundaries. The same would be true, over a much wider geographic area, of the Chernobyl disaster the same year, where a misguided attempt to test out the vulnerability of a nuclear reactor, nominally (and ironically) to ensure its safe and effective operation as part of the critical infrastructure, went tragically wrong, causing environmental, economic, social and health consequences, which remain issues of live concern today.

Europe has not suffered anything on the magnitude of the recent oil spill in the Gulf of Mexico in 2010, but that is no ground for complacency: Rather it should stimulate us to think critically about how Europe would respond to a similar crisis. Time spent on the 'what ifs' is rarely wasted.

Concepts of critical infrastructure are not uniform across Europe and are constantly evolving in line with rapid changes within European societies. A modern concept must embrace some of the enduring concerns while ranging more widely. To include any aspect of our modern life in a list of assets on which we rely and whose loss would be seriously disruptive is not sufficiently rigorous: we must include only those assets whose continued functioning – uninterrupted, meeting priority economic and public expectations – are really *critical* to societal wellbeing.

Concepts and definitions adopted by the European Union
Critical infrastructure vulnerability has been discussed and assessed within the European Union in accordance with a definition first proposed by the Commission as recently as 2004. This is essentially generic its conception:

> Critical infrastructure means an asset, system or part thereof located in Member States which is essential

for the maintenance of vital societal functions, health, safety, security, economic or social well-being of people, and the disruption or destruction of which would have a significant impact in a Member State as a result of the failure to maintain those functions.[1]

There are four points here of particular relevance to this chapter. The first is the recognition of a potentially adverse impact in a single European country. While that would be the most obvious manifestation of a threat to the critical infrastructure, such a threat would not necessarily be confined to one country alone and could easily spill across more than one, with the potential to affect most European countries to some degree. A failure of the banking system, of the kind which seemed a distinct possibility in October 2008, would have caused chaos across the whole of Europe and indeed worldwide.

Secondly, the context of this work has moved beyond terrorism alone to encompass risks related to terrorism and other security-related risks. That wider range recognises increased vulnerability inherent in the functioning of modern European societies. Thirdly, an explicit link is made between the assets constituting critical infrastructure and measures of prevention, preparedness and consequence management. Here again, a model adopted for the purposes of responding to terrorism has been developed to deal in specific terms, from the earliest stages right through to post-event, with a much wider range of scenarios, where the intended outcome is recovery from a serious or catastrophic event or occurrence.

Fourthly, expectations are set high: the policy aim is to provide 'measures aiming at upholding, and/or guaranteeing security and public order during a crisis situation'. Inherent in this aim is the recognition that damage to critical infrastructure might threaten security and public order. The test of the desired outcome, at its highest, is a guarantee of continued social functioning and order – a high hurdle to jump, but one that recognises the scale of potential risk. Hence the need to focus on what is really *critical*.

Linking generic concepts with specific sectors

Specific assets where loss, damage or degradation could have a critical impact will of course vary across individual European countries, but it is very likely that they would include some, if not all, of the following sectors: energy, food, water, transport, telecommunications, government and public services, emergency services, health and finance. Individual European countries might attach greater or lesser weight to each of these, disregard some and include others.

Five specific policy areas

Risk assessment: threats and hazards, both natural and man-made

A broad distinction can be drawn between natural and man-made threats. The latter are however much more complex, ranging from the activities of terrorists (the original driver) to include threats from serious crime, migration, environmental and climate change-issues, financial, industrial and economic threats, and many more.

Geographical threats

For natural risks (those whose occurrence is unrelated to specific human actions), the most obvious are catastrophic climate effects and other naturally occurring phenomena such as earthquakes, as discussed by Jeffrey Mazo in chapter 6. The earthquakes in central Italy in 2009 caused terrible loss of life and devastation in a large geographic area, with widespread damage to all aspects of the local civil infrastructure, both

Table 1: **Human/financial costs of European environmental events 2002–2008**

	Estimated Financial Cost	Fatalities
2002 Flooding in Central Europe	€18.5 billion	116
2003 Heatwave	€10 billion+	27,000
2005 Drought/Forest Fires in Iberia	$3.65 billion	58
2005 Floods in Romania	$1.6 billion	67
2005 Floods in Germany/ Switzerland/Austria	$3 billion	11
2007 Winter Storm Kyrill	$10 billion	49
2007 UK Floods	$8 billion	5
2007 Wildland Fires in Greece	$2 billion	67
2008 Winter Storm *Emma*	$2 billion	14
2008 Severe Storm *Hilal*	$1.5 billion	3

Source: Munich Re Topics Geo – Annual Review: Natural Catastrophes 2002, 2003, 2004, 2005, 2006, 2007, 2008

critical and non-critical. They were however confined to one European country, whose civil protection response had been long prepared for such an event, and for which European Union mechanisms were quickly triggered.

The flooding in Germany, Austria, the Czech Republic, Hungary and Romania in 2000, 2005 and 2006 was different, in that it affected more than one country and caused widespread damage to local transport, power, water, food distribution and other sectors, threatening the well-being of huge numbers of the civil population. It was unprecedented in its scale and severity and there is no guarantee that it will not happen again, despite the well-prepared civil-protection measures in countries at the heart of Europe. Poland suffered extensive flooding in May 2010.

Other countries, notably France in 2009, and the UK in 2006 and 2007, have suffered hurricane-scale storms and deluges causing extensive damage to power and water infrastructure, with consequent localised disruption. Table 1 shows the costs – in terms of fatalities and financial damage – of environmental crises in Europe from 2002 to 2008.

Nor should we overlook the immense damage which can be caused by the sea. In 2007, a storm surge in the North Sea threatened coastal defences in littoral states – Denmark, Belgium, the Netherlands and the UK. The Netherlands was particularly at risk because of its low-lying terrain, despite the extensive precautions implemented in the decades since the floods of 1953. But the European Flood Alert System, together with the national measures implemented as an act of national policy by the Government of the Netherlands, contained the damage to far less than had been feared.

However damaging natural events of this kind may prove to be, there will be a limit to the extent to which authorities can intervene, at least in the preventative sphere. The whole issue of climate change is relevant, though it is not the intention of this chapter to examine what linkages there may be between recent climatic events and climate change. Work on natural climatic disasters needs to proceed in close and sensitive alignment with work on climate change.

To this list of potential and actual natural threats must be added the volcanic eruptions in Iceland. It is unlikely that many European countries had included volcanoes in their risk registers before 2010. Yet Eyjafjallajökull and the vast ash cloud it generated caused one of the biggest and most costly disruptions to normal life in recent years. These issues will be examined in more detail later.

Biological threats
Biological hazards, whether originating with humans or with animals, are potentially extremely disruptive to the critical infrastructure. They can cause massive dislocation to the food chain, precipitating panic buying of food followed by shortages, with the bottom falling out of the market for certain commodities. This has effects on both transport and financial structures and can cause immediate pressures on health facilities. On a global scale, the food supply industry is critically

geared to 'just in time' deliveries which are highly sensitive to even temporary disruption, whether arising from a food scare or a hitch in the supply chain.

Where hazards originate from natural biological phenomena, the effects may be felt more directly on the staffing of critical infrastructure facilities such as health, food and transport outlets. Governments are becoming more successful in handling the prevention and preparedness aspects of these periodic crises, as the recent global response to the swine flu (H1N1) shows.

The swine flu crisis did not materialise, perhaps partly because the strain did not prove capable of mutating or killing healthy individuals who did not have pre-existing risk factors. However, the outbreak prompted questions about how swift and effective the response would be to a much bigger and faster-moving pandemic, rapidly crippling vital sectors of the critical infrastructure, from hospitals and clinics, through food and fuel production to industrial output. Furthermore, European states differ widely in the extent of their precautionary measures for triage, inoculation and quarantine.

Man-made risks
More significant is the work to scope man-made risks to the critical infrastructure. Terrorism, organised crime and illegal migration have harmful social effects, as well as an impact on critical infrastructure. Of these, terrorism is still probably the most worrying. Serious criminals seek to make profits with minimal impact upon the state and its institutions. Illegal migration, of the kind relentlessly experienced from North Africa by Italy and Spain, among others, threatens to cause social dislocation and to put burdensome demands on the critical infrastructure of power, water, food, energy, housing and health services, but the effects of such social pressures are

generally felt over a period of time, and to the extent that the pressures are immediate (such as a surge of boat people), they may well be localised. They do not usually precipitate collapse of critical infrastructure facilities even if they involve profound social, economic and demographic changes over time.

Terrorism

The threats from terrorism are altogether different. First of all, terrorists often seek to inflict mass casualties and damage, causing maximum impact with a single strike: the bigger the better. They operate on a global scale with an instant and worldwide reach and impact. The al-Qaeda attacks on Western cities have been designed to cause maximum casualties, indiscriminate in their choice of victims. The intention has been to paralyse major cities such as Berlin, Madrid, London and Paris and to induce fear in the civilian populations. The short-term aim was to cause dislocation of transport and other civil facilities (airports, urban railway and metro systems) with immediate effects in the demands on emergency facilities. The longer-term purpose was to induce fear and uncertainty in large urban populations, both indigenous and transient, and while it would be hard to claim that the effects on critical infrastructure were significant over time, the terrorists have challenged the security, stability and viability under pressure of key components of the critical infrastructure

One specific focus of concern is the extent to which the thinking of terrorist groups previously or currently active in Europe has targeted critical infrastructure as a direct weapon against the societies in those countries. In the UK, in 1996 an Irish Republican Army (IRA) plot to destroy the electricity supply to the Greater London area was foiled by police. More recently, the senior al-Qaeda plotter Khalid Sheikh Mohammed, now being held in Guantanamo Bay awaiting trial for war crimes, was believed in 2003 to have been planning an attempt to hijack aircraft leaving Heathrow Airport in London and crash them back onto the airport, which is responsible for some 8% of the UK's GDP. Such a plot would have fulfilled core al-Qaeda expectations of spectacular, multiple attacks causing maximum and indiscriminate casualties, as well as taking out, at least temporarily, an iconic and vital element in the UK's critical infrastructure.

Non-conventional weapons

Of greater worry is the long-standing interest of al-Qaeda in non-conventional weapons – chemical, biological, radiological and nuclear, or collectively CBRN – and their intent to acquire and use them. The Aum Shinrikyo sarin attack on the Tokyo subway in 1995 had longer-term effects on public confidence, in a vital part of the critical infrastructure in Japan's capital city, out of all proportion to its physical effects. The incident killed 12 and injured more than 5,000.

For Western governments, the near-ultimate nightmare is an attack using radiological material, in the form of a dirty bomb, where a small-scale conventional explosive device is used to distribute radioactive material over a wide area. While the effects in a rural area might not be immediately significant to food and water supplies, the impact on a major city would be devastating. Unseen and unfelt, such a toxic event would rapidly cause a major shut-down, entailing massive evacuation of both local residents and commuter workers, with direct and immediate impact on food, health, transport and energy sectors, soon extending to government, public services and financial and economic activity. The cosmopolitan nature of modern European cities and the lack of space to relocate people would place intense pressures on the resources needed to feed and shelter them.

More insidious would be the 'decapitation' effects on central political and financial structures. Much would depend on the extent to which planning in these sectors has factored in the consequences of a dirty bomb, for example in the provision of alternative sites, networks, facilities and staffing structures to meet the requirements envisaged in European planning in terms of consequence management measures, particularly their co-ordination.

Cyber attacks

These are the least understood and the most difficult to measure or predict, with widespread potential for major damage and enormous impact. The British government announced a new National Cyber Security Programme, worth some £650m, in October 2010 as part of its Strategic Defence and Security Review. Not surprisingly, cyber threats also figure significantly in European work programmes on Prevention, Preparedness and Consequence Management of Terrorism and Other Security Related Risks, reflecting the urgency and concern caused by current vulnerabilities.[2] The range of potential attackers is probably the most worrying aspect – including terrorists and organised criminals, nihilists and other global anarchists, through to state-sponsored attackers, with a wide range of motives. For present purposes, cyber attacks are taken to include telecommunications links more widely.

Delivering effective responses to the cyber threat is probably the most conceptually challenging task at the present time. A starting point must be an analysis of the current potential for damage and the risk that this would cause to systems, assets and people. Priority areas which have been identified are principally the Internet (including resilience to attack and interdependency modelling) and fixed and mobile communi-

Table 2: **EU Internet Access 2008**

	% of Households with Internet Access	% of Enterprises with Internet Access		% of Households with Internet Access	% of Enterprises with Internet Access
Austria	69	97	Latvia	53	88
Belgium	64	97	Lithuania	51	94
Bulgaria	25	83	Luxembourg	80	96
Cyprus	43	89	Malta	59	92
Czech Republic	46	95	Netherlands	86	99
Denmark	82	98	Poland	48	93
Estonia	58	96	Portugal	46	92
Finland	72	99	Romania	30	67
France	62	95	Slovakia	58	96
Germany	75	95	Slovenia	59	97
Greece	31	93	Spain	51	95
Hungary	48	86	Sweden	84	96
Ireland	63	96	UK	71	93
Italy	47	94	EU27	60	93

Source: Eurostat Statistics Database http://epp.eurostat.ec.europa.eu/portal/page/portal/statistics/search_database, (Accessed 4 July 2009)

cations (including priority use and restriction on data traffic when necessary).

Two requirements are of paramount importance: robustness under attack or heavy usage, and maintaining the capacity to communicate with the public. The involvement of the international information computer technology (ICT) sector, matching rapidly developing technological change to threat assessments, will be crucial, as well as robust exercising to test the extent to which critical infrastructure vulnerabilities can be prevented and damage mitigated. Table 2 shows just how much the public in European countries has come to use – and hence depend on – the Internet. The figures are even higher for commercial and industrial enterprises, with near universal coverage in some countries.

Industrial and economic risks
An obvious risk in these circumstances is the threat to energy supplies across Europe as a whole, such the recurrent winter-

Table 3: **EU Gas Storage Infrastructure June 2009***

	Gas Storage Capacity (mcm)		Gas Storage Capacity (mcm)
Austria	4,230	Latvia	2,000
Belgium	684	Lithuania	0
Bulgaria	350	Luxembourg	0
Cyprus	0	Malta	0
Czech Republic	2,321	Netherlands	5,078
Denmark	1,001	Poland	1,575
Estonia	0	Portugal	150
Finland	0	Romania	2,694
France	12,255	Slovakia	2,750
Germany	19,595.2	Slovenia	0
Greece	0	Spain	4,140
Hungary	3,720	Sweden	10
Ireland	0	UK	4,310.3
Italy	14,335	EU27	58,491.2

*Latvia from 2007
Source: GIE. Gas Investment Europe European Gas Storage Map, June 2009, http://www.gie.eu/maps_data/storage.html (Accessed 4 July 2009)

time difficulties in gas supplies reaching Europe via Ukraine, covered in more detail by Virginia Comolli (in chapter 8). Table 3 shows the widely differing gas-storage capacities across European countries as at June 2009. Equally difficult would be a threat, either man made or naturally occurring, to raw material supply, affecting either industrial capacity or availability of basic goods. The main impact of such problems would of course be upon producers and consumers rather than on fixed assets, and the effects would probably not be long lasting. But disruption of this kind nevertheless carries the capacity to cause some degradation of the critical infrastructure.

Volcanic ash

The fact that few European countries had paid much if any attention to the potential effects of the unfortunate confluence of an erupting Icelandic volcano and a predominantly northerly airflow shows the folly of concentrating solely on familiar risks. Volcanic eruptions are something that happens far away.

Yet for several days in April and May 2010 European communications, travel and commerce effectively came to a halt. The ash crisis demonstrated graphically, if it were needed, the vulnerability of critical infrastructure, how quickly problems can arise, how poor are the practices for assessing risk and taking operational decisions, and how much uncertainty there is when it comes to coordinating national and international response to a new problem.

We must now add airspace to our list of critical infrastructures, with the significant dimension that there is a limit to the scope of national solutions: you can fly through the airspace of several European countries in a matter of minutes – certainly in less time than it takes most European countries to activate their national crisis centres. The ash-cloud crisis should prompt action across a range of issues, but principally on the assessment of risk. It was clear that national air-traffic-control centres and major European airlines took radically different views of the risk to jet engines of flying through an ash cloud. Yet both claim passenger safety as their paramount concern, and rightly so. Why should their assessments differ so widely?

How can the work of vulcanologists, meteorologists, jet-engine manufacturers, air-traffic controllers, airport operators, commercial airlines, European transport ministries, and European aviation authorities be more closely aligned? All have a vital role to play in keeping Europe flying, and flying safely, but the public could be forgiven for feeling less than totally reassured, as the crisis unfolded, that all the main players were reading from the same script. There is clearly more urgent work to be done on the assessment of risk and on a range of mitigation measures, whether relating to air corridors, better predictions of ash-cloud movements, engine sensors or configuration of air schedules and public information. These are merely the issues which have come up in first reactions to the ash crisis. Above all, the ash soon became a global problem, not just a European one. Worldwide travel schedules were immediately disrupted, with knock-on effects across the globe, affecting tourists and business travellers and, to take an example of our interconnected world, Kenyan flower producers dependent on daily flights to Europe. As a global issue, some communities in some countries will have been much more affected than others. One estimate puts the cost to the airlines at over €2 billion.

What was lacking as the crisis unfolded was the capacity for thinking about the 'what ifs'. It was left largely to the media to speculate on what the impact might be, inevitably focusing on pictures of distraught holidaymakers in airport lounges. In those circumstances governments need groups of quick-thinking and imaginative minds, comprising both experts in the field and generic problem solvers, to scope – searchingly and rigorously – how the scenario of a sudden halt to air travel might impact upon economic and social life. From work of that kind can flow the immediate efforts to mitigate effects, to develop Plans B, C and more, and to regain the initiative. Such work is not costly, but it is urgent. The volcano may have settled down for now, but we have been taught a sharp lesson, and we need to learn from it both comprehensively and quickly.

Perception of risk across Europe

The starting point for European efforts in this field is a generic definition of critical infrastructure – what is really significant and critical, rather than sector or country specific. However, we can expect some variations. So as far as terrorism is concerned, those countries that have experienced terrorist attacks and threats will shape their preparations accordingly. The major victims have been Denmark, France, Germany, Greece, Italy, the Netherlands, Spain and the UK, although this list is not exhaustive. Some but not all of these countries, and others such as Poland, are associated in various degrees with NATO's efforts in Afghanistan, and to a lesser extent with the Iraq War. The closer the experience of terror, the greater is the likelihood of concern about the terrorist threat.

So far as other man-made threats are concerned, few European countries will have escaped anxiety, if nothing more, in the face of threats to energy supplies. All face widespread dislocation in the face of any generalised cyber threat of catastrophic proportions – even rural communities would be affected. European countries have already had to come to terms with the Chernobyl disaster in 1986 and its lasting effect on food and water supplies and health services. For other countries, the natural threats they encounter regularly or intermittently will figure largely in their planning. When the threats are exceptional, as in the case of the flooding in central Europe, costly mitigation planning may not be extensive, if the authorities calculate that the risk is not likely to bear immediate repetition.

Vulnerabilities of European countries

Perception is what governments fear could happen, based upon their experience and that of others. Vulnerability is more closely linked to a sharper assessment of the likely impact of any given set of events on critical infrastructure. To the extent that measures can be taken, vulnerability can be diminished. Those countries which see themselves in the eye of the terrorist threat have taken comprehensive steps to deal with it. Others may think that it won't happen to them, and in doing so risk increasing their vulnerability. Countries with strong resilience to energy disruption (e.g. in storage capacity for hydrocarbons) or robust preparations for alternative sources are less likely to suffer or to present a soft target. The same would be true where food-distribution systems rely less on 'just-in-time' deliveries and have some capacity for delay or redundancy.

Size or location are not much of a guide. Countries with larger populations or surface area generally require a proportionately larger critical infrastructure, but where those assets are robust and adequately protected, vulnerability can be diminished. To the extent that greater geographic size gives rise to greater regional or provincial autonomy, assets can be dispersed or diversified, thus enhancing local resilience. A small country or city-state needs to devote proportionately more of its resources to protecting its critical infrastructure in the face of multiple vulnerabilities: Singapore is a clear example.

Potential trends in threats

The governments of most countries usually ask their horizon-scanning teams to look ahead over fixed periods of time: five or ten years, or longer. While some European countries may view the ending of the Iraq War as removing an element of the AQ threat, those with a continuing presence in Afghanistan (such as the UK) will remain in AQ focus in the long term. On a longer view, those states presenting an obviously conspicuous set of liberal, democratic values based on a mature concept of human rights (such as Sweden) will remain a target, as will those where AQ feels that there are still scores to settle (Denmark and the Netherlands). Terrorists who take AQ ideology as an instrument to guide them think and plan on a far longer time-scale than a period of five or ten years. That brings into the frame a continued intent to develop CBRN weapons. Those states facing long-term domestic terrorist threats (Spain) will be planning to make progress dealing with the threat over a medium or long term, but would be hard placed to predict events accurately at this stage. As European societies grow ever more closely inter-linked, as economic and political moves are made towards greater integration, so the generalised vulnerabilities (cyber threats and energy shortages, the effects of climate change and a flu pandemic) can be expected to increase. How Europe deals with such threats depends to a large extent on how far action can be coordinated, and on how national measures of mitigation and defence can be joined up. In this respect it will be instructive to analyse further the extent to which measures across Europe to deal with the financial and economic crisis in 2008 were coordinated or were left to individual countries. The same is likely to be true when a full analysis is made of how eurozone countries handled the sovereign-debt problems in 2010.

The general planning assumption must be that – looking across the range of threats – they are more likely to increase than to diminish. Few could have predicted ten years ago the range of unexpected and unwelcome issues which Europe has had to deal with since then. Long gone are the hopes and certainties of the expected peace dividend after the collapse of the Berlin Wall. There are few indications that we are about to enter a more benign period. But European prosperity has advanced enormously in recent years, feeding public expectations that high levels of stability and plenty will be maintained. The stakes are high, both for national governments and for European institutions.

Policy recommendations

Drawing all this together, some important policy imperatives soon become clear. Some of these fall to European countries as nation-states, others can best be tackled using the whole weight and range of European institutions. At the macro level (high-level horizon scanning and policy planning), work needs to continue on the analysis of threats. This should be done over fixed time scales where this makes sense but should not be confined to them: if ever there was an area which needs to flourish without regard to boundaries, it is this. Work of this kind will need to start with threat assessments across the range, informed by the best professional advice for each sector. It should be based on a matrix pattern correlating the threat and the vulnerability, so as to create a meaningful assessment of risk.

Where steps have been taken to protect assets, their impact should be included in the assessment of vulnerability. In this way, progress towards mitigation can be measured and further resource allocations decided accordingly. There must continue to be a capacity for imaginative and far-reaching horizon scanning so that planning does not become stereotyped or limited by what has happened so far. Equally there must be some calibration of likelihood so that resources are not allocated to ephemeral or transitory threats. Here again, a matrix system will provide the best guide to the relative merits of projected expenditure on specific projects.

At the micro level, we can identify about 12 priority areas in European work programmes and research projects currently under way. These range from the behavioural (identifying individuals who pose security risks) to the directly physical (mitigation of blast effects). Many of them reflect concern about cyber threats and their secondary consequences (for example, the effect on the ability of governments to communicate with their citizens, and on individuals and communities to maintain communications links under attack, stress or degradation). Several of them acknowledge the important role of the private sector in protecting assets and guaranteeing resilience under pressure. Finally, the importance of exercising a wide range of scenarios, coordinating European actors, involving technical experts and promoting better understanding of major generic issues such as interdependencies, will remain key to future success.

CHAPTER SIX

Climate Change and Extreme Environmental Events

Jeffrey Mazo
Research Fellow for Environmental Security and Science Policy and
Managing Editor, *Survival*, IISS

Society has always been vulnerable to extreme environmental
events such as volcanic eruptions, earthquakes, freak weather
and ecological damage caused by human activity. Sometimes
the impact can be catastrophic: the ancient Minoan civilisation
of the Aegean was fatally weakened by earthquakes, ash fall and
tsunamis from an eruption – the largest in European history – of
the volcano Thera around 1450 BCE. Less catastrophically, ash
fall from volcanic eruptions in Iceland has been implicated in
numerous security-related events in European history, among
them a period of increased warfare in Bronze Age Scotland, a
series of crop failures that contributed to the French Revolution,
and the closure of parts of European airspace in April 2010.[1]
Extreme environmental events, by definition, are those lying
outside a society's normal experience, and hence often outside
that society's capacity to adapt.

By definition, too, extreme environmental events are
precisely those that are not to be *expected* during a particular
period, but where the probability of occurrence combined
with the potential harm creates sufficient risk that they must
be taken into account in planning and policymaking. They are

'black swans' or security wild cards, and thus impossible to predict reliably and difficult to plan for.[2] With the advent and acceleration of man-made global warming and consequent climate change, moreover, the frequency of many such events is already changing and will continue to do so at an ever-faster rate. European policymakers must be sufficiently aware of the potential impacts, likelihoods and overall risk of such events to be able to make informed judgements as to whether, how and to what degree to take them into account. Some hazards are so severe – for example a major asteroid impact – that the statistically defined risk is high despite the extremely low probability of occurrence in any meaningful timeframe. Others may have a much higher (if still relatively low) probability of happening in the next few decades, but the potential damage may be so low, or the existing capacity to cope with the events sufficiently robust, as to mitigate the risk. There is no simple way to identify priorities between types of events – in terms of developing the capacity to cope with their consequences – or between the need to allocate resources to such low-probability, high-impact events and more evident, long-term threats and trends.

Possible extreme environmental events over the next few decades pose a range of potential human-security and more conventional security threats to the European Union and its individual member states. While the frequency and severity of natural disasters globally has more than quadrupled in the last 50 years, Europe has been relatively blessed in this regard, experiencing fewer major events because of its geophysical circumstances as well as its ability to cope compared with most regions of the world.[3] In this context, 'disaster' is a socially determined concept: a major flood or earthquake in a sparsely inhabited region is not a catastrophe; the more robust and resilient a regional economy and society, the more severe an event has to be before it can be considered a disaster. Thus the same extreme environmental event may be considered a disaster in one particular time or place, but not in another. Yet, if highly resilient regions are pushed beyond the limits of their resilience, the consequences are more severe. European security is also affected by the economic, social and political impacts of environmental disasters in other regions.

Extreme environmental events may be divided into geophysical or tectonic events (volcanoes, earthquakes, landslides) and weather or climatic events (storms, floods, droughts, heat waves, unusual cold snaps). Some organisations, such as the UN Environment Programme, also consider major industrial accidents, such as the explosion and fire at the Chernobyl nuclear power plant in Ukraine in April 1986, as extreme environmental events. The direct impacts of such extreme environmental events may be societal, economic or environmental, and any of these can have further, indirect impacts. The resultant societal, geopolitical and economic consequences can in turn act as further drivers or threats to security.

Beyond their general chronic or acute systemic impacts, extreme environmental events can be threat multipliers for more traditional security concerns. Military forces, which are highly organised and prepared to act rapidly, are the only actors available to cope if the scale of a major domestic disaster exceeds the ability and resources of local or national emergency services. Disasters abroad can similarly create the need for humanitarian interventions beyond the scope of non-governmental organisations or civilian agencies, or exacerbate the conditions that give rise to the need for military interventions. Major events also have the potential to suddenly and dramatically alter the geopolitical balance in unpredictable ways.

Extreme tectonic and weather events

On 11 November 1755, an earthquake struck with an estimated magnitude of 9.0 on the Richter scale, equivalent to the energy of 32,000 1-megatonne bombs, in the Atlantic some 200km off the Portuguese coast. The resulting tremors, tsunami and fires almost completely destroyed the city of Lisbon, killing a fifth of its inhabitants. The total death toll in the Iberian Peninsula and North Africa has been estimated at around 50,000. It was not the first significant quake to strike the region; there had been at least 18 others in the previous 500 years. For comparative purposes, great quakes of this magnitude occur globally on average once every 20 years. (Every point on the Richter scale represents approximately 32 times as much energy released, and strong quakes of 6.0–6.9 or major quakes of 7.0–7.9 occur worldwide around 120 and 20 times a year respectively.)

Although quakes of such magnitude in the particular location that led to the destruction of Lisbon are only expected to occur on average every 3–4,000 years, the event is a stark example of the essentially unpredictable risk of major tectonic events in parts of Europe.[4] Of course, some geographical areas are at significantly greater risk than others, and the geological risks are reasonably well understood. But earthquakes can strike almost anywhere and at any time, and even relatively low-magnitude quakes can have devastating consequences in the immediate vicinity. A 7.2-magnitude quake that struck the city of Messina in Sicily on 28 December 1908 destroyed most of the city, generated a 12m tsunami and led to the loss of up to 200,000 lives on the island and on the Italian mainland. The twentieth century saw five other quakes of magnitude 6.5–7.9 in Italy that caused over 1,000 deaths. Modern building codes designed to minimise earthquake damage and loss of life, prompted in part by the Messina quake, have meant that earthquake casualties on the same order of magnitude as Lisbon or Messina have not recurred in Europe for nearly 100 years. But even the relatively modest 6.3-magnitude quake in L'Aquila in northern Italy on 6 April 2009 killed 307 people and made

66,000 homeless, and severely damaged a hospital built less than ten years previously to be earthquake-proof.

Romania is the only EU member state other than Italy that has experienced similar damage from earthquakes since 1900: in 1940 and 1977. Elsewhere in southeast Europe, Skopje in the Former Yugoslav Republic of Macedonia saw a 6.0 quake in 1963 that killed 1,100 people. In the wider European neighbourhood, Turkey has seen 17 quakes with death tolls of over 1,000 since 1900, including 1939 and 1999 temblors of magnitude over 7.5 and death tolls exceeding 10,000. Iran experienced 16 – including four, in 1962, 1968, 1978 and 1990, with tolls over 10,000 – and there were two large quakes in the Caucasus and three in North Africa.

It is statistically likely that Turkey and Iran will again experience large and damaging quakes between now and 2025, and it would not be surprising for such events to occur in Italy, southeastern Europe (including Greece and its islands), North Africa or the Caucasus. Great quakes of magnitude over 8.0 cannot be ruled out in any of these regions, particularly in Turkey or Iran. While a repeat of the 1755 Lisbon quake in Portugal (which could cost €12 billion) or anywhere else in Europe is extremely unlikely within this time frame, a much more modest and likely quake on a fault nearer to Lisbon could cause even more damage. The Alpine regions of France, Switzerland and Austria are also at some risk (the town of Basle was destroyed in 1356 by a quake thought to have been in excess of 6.0). But even areas considered low risk can still experience significant events: a 5.5 quake in the Netherlands in 1992 caused nearly €100m in damage.

The overall risk of earthquakes in different parts of the world is related to the underlying plate tectonics. While some types of plate boundary, such as those responsible for the large number of powerful quakes in Turkey and Iran, generate earthquakes only, others, such as those responsible for many of Italy's earth-quakes, are also associated with high levels of volcanic activity. The only active volcanoes in Europe, considered geographi-cally, are in Italy and its islands in the Mediterranean. Mt Etna in Sicily, for example, experiences relatively mild erup-tions with such frequency that they might not be considered extreme events, though they do cause periodic disruption to transportation, communications and other economic activity. There are, however, active volcanoes within EU territory else-where in the world: Montserrat (UK) and Guadaloupe (France) in the Caribbean, and the Azores (Portugal) in the Atlantic. The Canary Islands (Spain) and a number of Greek islands in the Aegean and Mediterranean have volcanoes that have seen eruptions in historical times.

Iceland, currently engaged in EU accession talks with a view to joining in 2012, is an entirely volcanic landscape, and its history more than that of any European state has been shaped by volcanic events. Explosive eruptions on scale of the one that began on 14 April 2010 at the sub-glacial Eyjafjallajökull volcano, occur in Iceland on average every 20–40 years, and given the right weather conditions the resultant ash cloud can reach Europe, with highly negative consequences – as indeed happened in this case.[5] Those consequences were indirect, stemming from the precautionary measures taken rather than the ash cloud itself, but more severe, if less frequent, eruptions have the potential to negatively impact Icelandic and European air quality, agriculture and livestock. An eruption of the Laki volcano in 1783 led to the deaths of 50% of Iceland's livestock (including 80% of its sheep) and up to 25% of the population. It caused thousands of deaths in Europe through atmospheric pollution and weather effects, and its climatic impact lasted for a decade, contributing to a series of famines that helped trigger the French Revolution.[6] Another volcanic eruption in

1875 devastated the Icelandic economy and, along with a series of unusually cold summers and stormy winters, led to the emigration of 20% of the population to North America.[7] That volcano, Askja, erupted again in 1961, and another eruption could be imminent.[8]

Until the 2010 Icelandic eruption, the best example of how such a threat could affect Europe – and the most likely – was Mt Vesuvius, near Naples. Events on the scale of the eruption of 79 CE, which buried the towns of Pompeii and Herculaneum, have happened only four times in the last 20,000 years, but the mountain continued to erupt around every 100 years until 1037. It was then quiescent until 1631, when it underwent a violent eruption – in general, the longer the period between eruptions, the more violent the subsequent event. The mountain continued to erupt frequently until 1944, but has been quiet since then. The 1631 eruption is considered the worst-case scenario for a new eruption. However, since 1944 the population has grown and development has spread, and there are now over 600,000 people living in the area considered to be under serious threat and who will require evacuation in the event of a new eruption. Current evacuation plans require two weeks' warning,[9] but even if the plans work perfectly a major eruption would cause widespread damage and economic disruption, and the long lead-time increases the chance of false alarms. Efforts are under way to reduce the required warning to two to three days within 20–30 years.[10]

The ash cloud from the 2010 Icelandic volcano, which had last erupted in 1821–23, led to the closure of parts of European airspace for six days. At one point, air traffic fell below 20% of the usual level, and intermittent travel disruption lasted for some weeks afterwards. More than 100,000 flights were cancelled, 10m passengers were stranded and the estimated economic impact, including direct costs to airlines and other aviation-related sectors, ranged from €1.5–2.5bn.[11] This figure does not include the economic impact of delayed arrival of passengers and goods. The Icelandic eruption was particularly bad because its sub-glacial nature created 'the wrong kind of ash', and weather conditions that occur only 6% of the time carried that ash into European airspace.[12] Europe continues to face volcanic ash hazards, however, not just from Iceland but from the Azores, the Canary Islands, Italy and the Aegean.

Unlike tectonic events, which are discrete and violent departures from everyday experience, some extreme weather events can only be defined statistically as variations from the norm. Weather-related events such as major floods are like tectonic events in this regard. A period of sustained high temperatures moreover can be considered a heat wave, for example, if those temperatures are unusual for that season and that location, whereas identical weather could be considered normal in a different region. As will be discussed later in this chapter, climate change, even within the 2025 time horizon, may increase the frequency of events that would now be considered extreme, to the point that they would be considered within the *normal* range. However, what is extreme and what is not is also a question of how well society is able to cope with the event, and this goes right to the issue at hand. Unless and until European societies are able to adjust or adapt to a changed, more severe climate, there will be security consequences, and the necessary adaptations will themselves have security implications. Moreover, one of the necessary adaptation mechanisms will be security policy itself. For present purposes extreme weather events will be considered against twentieth-century norms.

In summer 2003, for example, Europe as a whole experienced its hottest summer since 1780 (the first year for which there are adequate records) with average temperatures 1.4°C higher than the second hottest (1807) and 3.8°C higher than the late twentieth-century mean. Many places in France, Germany, Italy, Spain, Switzerland and the UK recorded their highest-ever single temperatures, beating records set in the 1940s or 1950s. The high temperatures were sustained throughout the month of August, and many parts of Western and Central Europe saw little or no rainfall. The impacts were severe: total EU wheat production fell by 10%, transport systems were disrupted, power plants were forced to shut down and there were an estimated 35,000 excess deaths.[13] France was particularly badly affected. Less severe but nonetheless significant and unusual heatwaves struck Europe in 2006 and early summer 2009. In 2010, Europe along with other parts of the northern hemisphere, experienced another severe heatwave, with many countries again seeing record high temperatures. It was at its worst and most prolonged in Eastern Europe and Russia, where it caused over 10,000 excess deaths in Moscow alone, destroyed more than a quarter of the grain harvest and cost the Russian economy $7–15bn.[14] The resulting drop in Russian exports pushed global wheat prices up steeply. One estimate put the global cost of the price increases at $67bn.[15] The overall human and economic cost was of the same order of magnitude as the Chernobyl nuclear accident.

The reverse of the heatwave is the cold snap. Sudden or extended periods of below-average temperatures can have similar impacts, including excess mortality, disruption to transportation, damage to infrastructure and agriculture, and spikes in energy demand that can overload infrastructure and lead to shortages and energy insecurity. Europe experienced three such widespread snaps in the five years to 2010: winter 2004–05 mainly in Southern Europe, winter 2005–06 mainly in Eastern Europe, and winter 2008–09. Even in countries where society has adapted to routinely low winter temperatures, cold snaps can cause disruption and health impacts. In unprepared countries these can be much more severe.

Similarly, although heatwaves are generally associated with drought conditions and vice versa, extreme precipitation events can also have severe impacts, notably flooding. In August 2002, for example, Austria, the Czech Republic, Germany and Italy saw widespread and severe flooding due to two discrete heavy rainfall events. Slovakia, Slovenia, Spain and the UK were also affected. There were over 100 deaths throughout Europe, and in the four worst-affected countries over 300,000 people were evacuated and total damage and economic impact was estimated to have been €20–25bn.[16] There were localised floods in 2005 and 2007, and in June 2009, again, Austria, the Czech Republic, Germany, Hungary, Poland, Romania and Slovakia were badly hit by floods, although damage assessments had not yet been completed at the time of writing. Similar widespread precipitation-induced flooding took place in northern Europe (France, Germany and the low countries) in 1993 and 1995. Localised (national-scale or smaller) flooding events of comparable severity are even more frequent. The 2010 heatwave lead to severe flooding in Germany and Poland.

Severe flooding can also be the result of storm surges, when high winds and high tides combine to flood low-lying coastal areas, as happened with the US city of New Orleans during Hurricane Katrina in 2005. On the night of 31 January 1953, a major storm in the North Sea combined with high spring tides to raise water levels in many places by more than 2.5m above mean sea level, and up to 5.5m in some locations, causing extensive flooding in the Netherlands and the UK and affecting parts of the Belgium, France and Denmark. There were at least 1,800 deaths in the Netherlands and more than 300 in the UK, and over 10% of Dutch agricultural land was flooded. London was only saved from flooding because sea walls failed elsewhere, diverting the water; and millions of people in the provinces of North and South Holland were similarly saved only by ad hoc emergency repairs to the Dutch sea defences.

In response to the 1953 flood disasters, the government of the Netherlands began construction of an ambitious system of flood defences, only completed in 1997 at an estimated total cost of €5bn. To protect its capital, the UK built the Thames Barrier, completed in 1982 at a cost of £1.3bn. Although these defences have been employed many times, their true value was demonstrated in November 2007 when there was a coincidence of a powerful (but not extraordinary) storm and a spring tide similar to the 1953 event. The surge in 2007 was only about 0.5m less than the one in 1953. According to the UK Environment Agency it came to within 10cm, 'a hair's breadth', of breaching the sea defences. If the storm had been delayed by only three hours until high tide, however, it would have been much worse.[17] With the threat of increased frequency of storms, and rising sea levels due to global warming, the Thames Barrier and the Dutch system are already considered inadequate according to their original risk specifications, and improvements are planned.

Climate as a threat multiplier

For the purposes of policy planning, the likelihood of tectonic events in particular locations can be considered fixed, although there may be a greater or lesser degree of uncertainty in the scientific understanding of those likelihoods; however, the events can be considered essentially random within those frequency parameters. For extreme weather events, however, there is a wild card: global warming and consequent climate change due to human activity, in particular vastly increased (and increasing) emissions of carbon dioxide (CO_2) and other 'greenhouse gases' since the beginning of the industrial revolution. The frequency and severity of extreme weather events may both increase significantly in the years to 2025, with consequences for European security. It is never possible to attribute any individual event to climate change, only long-term patterns. Climate is, by definition, weather averaged over 20 or 30 years. Thus, although it is plausible, even likely, that the increased flood risk Europe has been experiencing in the past decade is in part due to climate change, it will be some time before this can be confirmed statistically. In some cases, however, such as the historically unprecedented 2010 Russian heatwave, there are plausible mechanisms predicted by climate models that connect them with global warming.[18]

In February 2007 the physical sciences working group of the Intergovernmental Panel on Climate Change (IPCC) reported that global warming, which had averaged 0.13°C per decade over the previous 50 years, would continue over the next two decades at nearly twice that rate, regardless of which set of assumptions were taken for trends in greenhouse-gas emissions.[19] Even if the increase in concentrations of greenhouse gases in the atmosphere could be stopped entirely, warming would still continue at about half that rate. The historical trend in Europe is considerably higher than the global mean, especially in central and northeastern Europe and mountainous regions, but it is lower in the Mediterranean.

The nature of the IPCC reporting process and a number of studies and summaries published more recently all suggest that, if anything, the IPCC projections underestimate the amount, rate and impact of anthropogenic climate change.[20] On the other hand, this smoothed projected trend obscures a high degree of potential variability. The difference in weather – temperature or precipitation – can be substantially greater from one year to the next than any underlying climate change. The World Meteorological Organisation, for example, uses 30-year averages to identify climate trends.

Besides random or chaotic fluctuations, there are also cyclical weather patterns on various timescales that are also subject to variations in timing and severity. The most important of these is a two- to seven-year cycle of fluctuation in the El Niño–Southern Oscillation system, a coupling of global-scale tropical and sub-tropical atmospheric pressure patterns with tropical Pacific surface temperatures. A period of anomalously high sea-surface temperatures in the tropical Pacific is called an 'El Niño', its colder twin is a 'La Niña'. These can have widespread effects on temperature and precipitation patterns. An apparent levelling-off of global warming in the last decade is an artefact of a strong El Niño in 1998, exemplifying the need to consider climate over multi-decadal periods. Only in the last few years have scientists begun to investigate the feasibility of producing useful medium-term forecasts. One research group suggests that over the next decade variations in oceanic circulation in the North Atlantic could produce sufficient cooling in Europe, North America and the tropical Pacific to temporarily offset the warming trend from greenhouse emissions. Another group achieved similar results, but they suggest a temporary slowing down rather than reversal of warming over the next decade.[21]

Beyond such impacts, which are expected to increase in severity in line with increasing temperatures globally or regionally, there is a potential for sudden, non-linear impacts such as abrupt sea-level rise or regional cooling through shutdown of warm ocean currents such as the Gulf Stream caused by the infusion of cold, fresh meltwater from melting ice caps. These potential impacts are abrupt in the sense that they occur much faster than the underlying temperature changes that induce them, but they would nevertheless be expected to take anywhere from a decade to a century or more to reach full effect. None of these non-linear impacts is considered likely in this century, let alone in the next decade or two, but the level of confidence of such projections is low and the consequences are particularly high.

Direct impacts of climate change in Europe, considered as an environmental event in its own right, include increased flooding, drought and fire risk, water stress, vector-borne disease and ecological disruption. Regional differences will be magnified: the north will see increased precipitation, water availability and crop and forest productivity, with the south experiencing opposite trends. There will be greater winter warming in the north and summer warming in central and southern Europe. Many of these effects are only likely to fully manifest outside the 2025 time horizon. The most significant effect of global warming over the next two decades will be an increase in the variance, rather than the mean, of temperature and precipitation. This means that, while average temperatures will continue to increase, and average rain- or snowfall will change regionally, the variation around this average will also increase. Rather than a discernable pattern of 'normal' weather with infrequent extreme events, there will be more periods of both abnormally high and low temperatures, and abnormally high or low rainfall. In other words, extreme weather events will tend to become the norm. Even if some extremes such as cold snaps become less severe, they will become more frequent. Other events will increase in both frequency and severity.

The perception of risk in Europe

The perception of the threat of extreme environmental threats among policymakers and the general public varies from country to country within Europe. Even before the global financial crisis and recession, only 5% of Europeans listed the environment as one of the two most important issues facing their country (the number was fairly consistent across Europe, except in Scandinavia, where it was considerably higher). A 2007 Eurobarometer report[22] showed that the percentage of respondents who said that protecting the environment was very important to them personally ranged from 94% in Cyprus to 47% in Finland, and numbers saying it was not very important or unimportant ranged from 1% to 8%. However, in the EU as a whole, extreme events only just made the list (tied at 32% with the health impact of chemicals used in daily life) when people were asked to pick the five main environmental issues that worried them. The survey did not distinguish between weather and tectonic events, but rather asked about 'natural disasters (earthquakes, floods etc.)'. Chronic water and air pollution (42% and 40% respectively), and man-made disasters such as oil spills or industrial accidents (39%) were of much greater concern. Climate change topped the list at 57%, up from 45% in 2004, a reaction to the increased publicity given the issue by the release of former US Vice President Al Gore's 2006 Academy Award-winning documentary film *An Inconvenient Truth*, the 2007 IPCC report, and the awarding of the Nobel Peace Prize jointly to Gore and the IPCC. There is, nevertheless, no indication that there is detailed public awareness of the particular risks of increased extreme weather events due to climate change; most popular public discourse still reflects a perception of climate change as synonymous with global warming, and global warming conceived as linear rather than as an averaged trend.

Within the EU, citizens of the UK and the Scandinavian countries felt themselves the most informed on environmental issues, followed by Western Europeans. Citizens of southern and southeast European countries, including the newer member states, felt themselves the least informed, and the gap had significantly widened between 2004 and 2007. The distribution of countries whose citizens saw climate change as one of the most important environmental issues tended to follow an east–west rather than north–south pattern, while the pattern of those more likely to list natural disasters among their greatest environmental concerns mirrored the pattern of extreme weather events across Europe in the previous five years. The results suggest that Europeans' perceptions of environmental risks tend to reflect chronic or immediate problems rather than longer-term threats of extreme events.

There are few data on perceptions of more specific environmental risks and threats. It might be expected that for tectonic events, for example, where the risk varies widely between countries, populations in regions that frequently experience minor or insignificant, but nevertheless perceptible, quakes would be more aware of the dangers. But in fact the risk in many parts of Europe appears to be so far below the threshold of awareness that the question is not even asked. England, for example, experiences a 5.0 quake every 10–20 years, whereas Italy had nine in a single three-month period in 2009 alone. The public reaction and tone of the media coverage when a 5.5 quake struck Lincolnshire in England in 2008 suggests that there is little or no public awareness or understanding of the risks.

Paradoxically, unusually cold winter weather in Europe in 2009–10, an extreme entirely consistent with climate projections and global warming, may have contributed to a decline in the percentages of the public that believe climate change is real, a serious threat and due to human activity.[23] This loss in confidence in the science was also, however, a result of a series of widely reported allegations of errors and malfeasance in the IPCC assessment process and reports. While these allegations were not in the end borne out,[24] their effect on public perception was real. Two in particular dealt with the impact of extreme environmental events in Europe and elsewhere. The first involved the question, discussed above, of attribution of natural disasters to climate change and the identification of an upwards trend in economic losses.[25] The second involved an error in the figure for how much of the Netherlands lies below sea level. This figure came from the Netherlands Environmental Assessment Agency, was superficial and in any case had no bearing on the IPCC's conclusions about the risk of flooding.[26] Although the scientific consensus on climate change remained robust, the reports and responses to the allegations did not receive the same media attention as the allegations themselves, and the damage to public perception had been done.

At the level of national security policymaking, however, there is greater awareness of the threats. Many European countries, including France, Germany and the UK have explicitly included climate change or environmental degradation in recent assessments of threats and drivers, usually in the context of generating instability outside Europe. Most European countries at least see the need to participate in crisis-management missions as an important driver of their defence policies.[27] Beyond the defence community, Europe has been driven by human- and national-security considerations to take the lead in international climate-change mitigation negotiations, and through the example of EU climate policy.

Security threats

Extreme environmental events clearly pose direct threats to human security and well-being, but they can contribute directly and indirectly to more traditional security threats. A 2008 report to the European Council on climate change and international security from the European Commission and Secretary-General/High Representative notes that climate change 'beyond 2°C will lead to unprecedented security scenarios' stemming from conflict over resources, economic damage and risk to coastal cities and critical infrastructure, border disputes, environmentally induced migration, instability in weak and failing states, tension over energy supply, and pressure on international governance.[28] While even under worst-case projections it is unlikely that warming will reach such levels until well after 2050, and the impacts will take even longer to play out, some of these security impacts will begin to manifest in response to levels of warming and degrees of climate change expected before 2025.

The global economic impact of extreme environmental events would be likely to continue to increase simply in response to increased population and prosperity, even in the absence of climate change. Europe has historically felt relatively mild effects from extreme environmental events compared to other regions that are either more at risk or less able to cope. Costs – whether from damage or from the expense of adaptation – will rise, however, as extreme weather events become both more frequent and more extreme. This will be in addition to the cost of measures to mitigate climate change, without which the critical impact threshold will be reached sooner or exceeded further. While this can be considered a long-term security imperative, it means fewer resources will be available for other priorities, including traditional security forces and structures.

Both extreme tectonic and weather events can damage critical infrastructure, including industrial plant, energy generation and transport systems and defence installations, many of which are sited in low-lying areas at particular risk of flooding. The damage may increase at a greater rate than the increase in frequency and severity of extreme weather events. For example, in the 2002 floods in Central Europe there was relatively little damage to major industrial plants compared to residential buildings, since efforts to protect them were a priority both for their economic importance and to prevent further environmental pollution in the event of damage. If more severe events exceeded the threshold beyond which they could be protected, the increased impact would be exponential rather than linear.

Besides the threat of direct damage to energy infrastructure, extreme environmental effects can affect energy security by, for example, putting stress on systems through spikes in demand for electricity in response to unusual weather; at the same time the weather causes temporary disruption in supplies. In 2003, 2006 and 2009, heatwaves forced the shutdown of nuclear power plants in several European countries, notably France. Although the resulting shortfalls could be made up by importing energy from neighbouring countries, longer, more severe or more widespread heatwaves in future, coupled with an increased reliance on nuclear power as part of a low-carbon economy, could turn the problem from an inconvenience to a real threat.

Military resources are often called on to assist civil response in the event of natural disasters, since they already exist for defence purposes, whereas dedicated civilian disaster-response is more expensive to maintain. In the floods in 2009, for example, the Czech Republic called out 1,000 soldiers to assist in the response – as many as are deployed abroad in NATO or EU peacekeeping missions. Using the military in such roles places more of a strain on, but is not limited to, smaller nations, especially since the climate change factors affecting extreme environmental events within Europe will also contribute to an increase in situations where troops might need to be deployed abroad. Recent proposals for an enhanced European Emergency Response Capability would improve coordination and efficiency of national disaster response, both civilian and military, including through Common Security and Defence Policy mechanisms, but would not provide any additional resources.[29]

While severe extreme tectonic events within the European Union are less likely than not to occur within in the 2025 time horizon, the probability is greater in Europe's immediate neighbourhood. A major earthquake in the Balkans could have significant consequences for political development and EU or NATO deployments in the region. A major earthquake in Turkey could create social and political instability on Europe's doorstep. A similar event in the geopolitical hotspots of the Caucasus or Iran could create sudden crises or shifts in the regional balance of power.

Such scenarios could impact on European energy security through disruption of energy infrastructure such as the planned Nabucco and Trans-Caspian gas pipelines and their intermediate links that will transport Central Asian gas from Turkmenistan to Central Europe, reducing Europe's critical dependence on Russia. An earthquake could damage the pipeline or related infrastructure directly, or contribute to social and political conditions that might interfere with gas supply.

An extreme weather event, major volcanic eruption or, more likely, an earthquake or tsunami elsewhere in the world could have a global economic impact or change the global geopolitical balance, with security consequences for Europe. The direct impact of Hurricane Katrina on the US economy and energy infrastructure serves as an example of how an extreme weather event in Europe might similarly impact European interests. But the aftermath of Katrina also had a direct effect on global energy prices, and its effect on the US economy had secondary ramifications for the rest of the world. More such storms, or an earthquake that devastated a major financial centre in a tectonically active zone, such as Los Angeles or Tokyo, could deliver a shock to the international financial system similar to or greater than that created by the terrorist attacks on New York on 11 September 2001. China, too, is at risk of major earthquakes, and anything that might affect its rapid economic emergence would have geopolitical consequences. Similarly, a storm or quake could affect critical manufacturing facilities outside Europe, particularly East Asian semiconductor facilities. The 1999 7.6-magnitude Taiwan earthquake, for example, temporarily disrupted global supplies of memory chips.

Both extreme weather events and long-term climate change considered as such an event in its own right could lead to land, water and food scarcity in many regions, particularly in sub-Saharan Africa. The consequences could include environmentally induced large-scale migration, including to Europe. This would either place increased demands on resources within the EU, or on militaries and border security agencies to keep illegal immigrants from arriving. Moreover, extreme environmental events and resource scarcity could create instability in many regions that would be exacerbated by internal and cross-border migration within the region. The conflict and instability thus created could mean an increased need for interventions by European forces and civilian missions. The unusually severe monsoon rains and consequent flooding in Pakistan in July–August 2010 created just such conditions in a region where European militaries are already engaged, and where many terrorist threats to Europe originate.[30] The flooding was connected to the same unusual weather pattern that lay behind the Russian heatwave.[31]

None of these potential security effects of extreme environmental events stands on its own. There are multiple synergies between and among them, and the more severe the event, the more likely that these synergies will multiply the effects. Nevertheless, there are two major strands to the threat presented by extreme environmental events: the abrupt, game-changing consequences of unforeseeable individual events, and systemic stresses created by climate change, including increased frequency and severity of such events. This latter dynamic is, indeed, the basis for the categorisation of climate change as a 'threat multiplier' in the 2008 European Commission/High Representative report on climate change and international security.[32] The report concludes that the EU should improve its capacity to prevent, and prepare for early responses to, climate-related conflicts and disasters. This could include intensifying capacities for basic research and analysis; and enhancing monitoring and early-warning capabilities as well as civil and military crisis-management and disaster-response instruments.

Responses and policy approaches

The community that builds blithely on the slopes of an active volcano, blissfully ignoring the ticking time bomb beneath it, is a classic literary trope. Although there is awareness at local, national and European levels of the threat of extreme environmental events, all too often the low probability of specific events leads to an 'out of sight, out of mind' mentality. And some threats are not anticipated: the effects of the ash cloud from the Icelandic volcano on the European transport system and economy in April 2010 came as a surprise. What national mechanisms and contingency plans were in place proved to be inadequate to the task, and the uncoordinated response and application of different standards across national borders contributed to the problem. It illustrates the point that the more unlikely an event, the less prepared European governments are likely to be – for good reason, given the need to prioritise scarce resources – and thus the risk is actually increased.

By their nature as extraordinary events, the extreme phenomena discussed in this chapter are particularly difficult to plan for. Since the timing and severity of extreme environmental events will always be unknowable, preparation, adaptation and systemic resilience are critical. In one respect, preparation for such events is, like investment in military forces and capabilities, a form of insurance against circumstances which it is to be hoped will never occur. But military capabilities also serve a second function of deterrence; investment in this sector can thus help prevent unwanted outcomes. Most extreme environmental events cannot be prevented, although their impacts may be ameliorated by appropriate measures. Extreme precipitation events, for example, are unavoidable, but whether they lead to flooding in places where it can affect human or economic security depends on the infrastructure in place. In the longer term, on a scale of five or more decades, appropriate measures to limit or reduce greenhouse gas emissions and mitigate climate change could have a preventative effect. Climate change is the wild card in assessing potential threats from extreme environmental events, and mitigation is the first line of defence. Emissions targets within Europe should be vigorously pursued and European states should continue to press for a strict and effective global emissions regime. Given limited resources, exacerbated by the global financial crisis, a balance must be struck between investment against environmental and other security threats and drivers in Europe as well as, in the case of threats driven by climate change, between preventative (mitigation), resilience and sectoral adaptation measures.

Priority should be given to investment in infrastructure, such as the upgrading of flood defences currently planned in the UK and the Netherlands, and the retrofitting of buildings to improve earthquake resistance. Diversification of sources and transportation systems for energy and other critical resources should be encouraged to minimise disruption in the event of damage or interference. Along the same lines, climate-change projections should be taken into account in all planning processes for new construction or development at all levels of government from the EU to national and local and across all sectors to improve resilience. Structuring of insurance schemes should discourage building in zones at particular risk of extreme environmental events, now or due to future climate change. Current zoning laws and building codes should be strictly enforced and anti-corruption measures strengthened.

Extreme environmental events, more than many other security threats, require robust and detailed scientific understanding to evaluate properly. Funding for basic geological and climate research, earthquake and volcano prediction, climate projections and related science should be maintained at least at current levels at national and EU levels, if not increased. This will be difficult in the current economic climate, with pressure on national budgets and the prospect of cuts across the board. Although such cuts are necessary, and the burden must be shared across sectors, they should be implemented in such a way as to minimise the damage in the long term. Postponing investment in particular projects is one thing, but cuts that affect the knowledge base that will allow such investment in future could be disastrous.

As Robert Whalley points out in the preceding chapter, the earthquakes in central Italy in 2009 which caused widespread infrastructure damage were confined to a single country with long-prepared civil protection response mechanisms, and for which an EU response was quickly triggered. Likewise, after 2003 many European countries adopted national emergency plans specifically designed for heatwaves. But in other cases the threat is transnational, as with the floods in 2000, 2005 and 2006 that affected more than one country and threatened the well-being of large numbers of people. Much current research and monitoring of tectonic risks and hazards is done at national level, and the response to the Icelandic volcano was hampered by different national standards and systems. Plans for an EU air network manager to facilitate decision-making and coordinate national responses were fast-tracked after the Icelandic eruption, but they will still leave decisions in the hands of national authorities. Such increased coordination, as well as communication and interaction between EU member states should be actively supported and encouraged. Similarly, communications between security- and environmentally oriented civil-society organisations and the environmental and security policy communities within and between EU member states, and other European countries, should be improved.

The extent of public awareness of particular environmental threats is not fully clear, but it appears to be inadequate. While more survey data needs to be collected, there should also be public awareness campaigns throughout Europe, targeted appropriately at particular countries and particular risks, such as earthquake awareness in Portugal and Southeast Europe. Public understanding of science in general is also inadequate, and for climate change especially, education and information provision need to be improved.

As extreme environmental events contribute to both direct and indirect traditional security threats, the effects of climate change should be taken into account in any future elaborations of the Common Security and Defence Policy, and in the planning of national defence structures and institutions, to ensure they are able to cope with anticipated developments. This must be informed, in particular, by a better understanding than currently exists of expected short- to medium-term climate change (on the scale of a few decades) as well as regional projections. Such research has a real security component: whereas the security impacts of long-term climate change are an argument for early mitigation to prevent them rather than for a security response, the more modest climate change that is inevitable over the next few decades will directly affect the security environment.

Extreme environmental events, whether in Europe or else-where in the world, are perhaps less direct threats to European security than others discussed in this book. They can have an impact on such threats and trends in areas such as energy or critical infrastructure, and their more general systemic effects can contribute to many of the others. But it is the non-linear nature of the more severe events, as potential game-changers or wild cards, which pose both the greatest threat to security and the greatest challenge to those who must anticipate, miti-gate and avoid their effects. This same trait tends to make them a lower priority for policymakers than some others. This may be justified given the relative probabilities and impacts, but if threats are downplayed, overlooked or ignored, the risks may turn out to be greater.

CHAPTER SEVEN

WMD Proliferation

Ben Rhode
Research Associate for Non-Proliferation and Disarmament, IISS

The European Union has described the proliferation of weapons of mass destruction (WMD) as 'potentially the greatest threat' to its security.[1] Although the EU's member states and some of its institutions have been involved in non-proliferation activities for many years, the September 2001 attacks on the United States and the policy divisions prior to the American-led invasion of Iraq in March 2003 brought into sharp focus the need for a coherent and comprehensive European strategy to prevent the proliferation of WMD to both states and non-state actors. The Iraq War revealed fault lines within the EU, as countries such as Italy, the Netherlands and the United Kingdom (among others) sided with the American policy to disarm Iraq through forced regime change, while France, Germany and others did not. The crisis highlighted the importance of adopting a coherent policy against WMD proliferation that would be acceptable to all member states, and would eschew the unilateral, strongly military approach against WMD proliferation of the George W. Bush administration embodied in its National Security Strategy of 2002, yet remain effective in addressing what all agreed was a serious threat.

Javier Solana, the high representative for the Common Foreign and Security Policy (CFSP), presented his draft European Security Strategy (ESS) in June 2003. It was accompanied by the 'Basic Principles for an EU Strategy Against Proliferation' and the 'Action Plan for the Implementation of [the Basic Principles]'. These were adopted by the General Affairs and External Relations Council. The European Council's Presidency Conclusions at Thessaloniki on 19–20 June included as an annex the 'Declaration on Non Proliferation of Weapons of Mass Destruction' that described the proliferation of WMD and their means of delivery as a 'growing threat to international peace and security',[2] and committed the EU to elaborate a coherent EU strategy before the end of 2003 that would draw on the Basic Principles. In October that year, Solana created the post of his personal representative on nonproliferation of WMD.[3] In December 2003 the final version of the European Security Strategy (ESS), *A Secure Europe in a Better World*, was released. A more detailed associated document published alongside the ESS, entitled the 'EU Strategy Against Proliferation of Weapons of Mass Destruction' (henceforth known as the WMD Strategy), drew on the publications from earlier that year. While these strategies and their accompanying review documents and reports are concerned with a broad range of proliferation-related issues and threats, in recent years the most obvious challenge to the EU's non-proliferation policy, and to the broader non-proliferation regime itself, has been posed by the Iranian nuclear crisis.

What is the EU worried about?

The ESS identified WMD proliferation as one of the 'key threats' to Europe, alongside terrorism, regional conflicts, state failure and organised crime. It went so far as to describe it as 'potentially the greatest threat to our security', and argued that '[we are] entering a new and dangerous period that raises the possibility of a WMD arms race, especially in the Middle East'.[4] The WMD Strategy warned that the proliferation of weapons of mass destruction was a 'growing' threat that 'puts at risk the security of our states, our peoples and our interests around the world' and that, despite the success of treaty regimes and export controls in slowing proliferation, 'a number of states have sought or are [sic] seeking to develop such weapons'.[5] It goes on to warn that such proliferation of WMD increased the likelihood that they would eventually be used, and identifies an increased threat to expatriate European communities, deployed troops and economic interests (natural resources, investments and export markets) in regions where WMD programmes are being developed.

The ESS identified nuclear activities in North Korea, nuclear risks in South Asia, and nuclear proliferation in the Middle East as major threats to European interests. However, while acknowledging that the proliferation threat is global and requires a global approach, the WMD Strategy underlines that Europe's security is especially linked to the stability and security of the Mediterranean, and that particular attention should therefore be paid to the potential for proliferation in the Mediterranean. In practical terms, this reflects the vital significance of Iran's proliferation activities, given their impact on the security of the eastern Mediterranean and the potential for a proliferation cascade in the region.

In addition to the challenge of state proliferation, the WMD Strategy stressed that the risk of terrorist acquisition of WMD 'adds a new critical dimension to this threat'.[6] The ESS described it as 'the most frightening scenario', as a small group would then be able to inflict damage that had previously only been within the reach of national armies. In this way, the ESS framed its discussion of new security challenges within the context of globalisation and technological advances: new technologies combined with increased cross-border flows had amplified the threat posed by non-state actors. The WMD Strategy warned:

> the potential for the misuse of … dual-use technology and knowledge is increasing as a result of rapid developments in the life sciences. Biological weapons are particularly difficult to defend against … The consequence of the use may be difficult to contain … They may have particular attractions for terrorists. Biological weapons, as well as chemical weapons, pose a special threat in this respect.[7]

To improve the efficiency of the WMD Strategy through greater EU coordination, the document *New Lines for Action by the European Union in Combating the Proliferation of Weapons of Mass Destruction and their Delivery Systems* (henceforth referred to as 'New Lines') was published in 2008. It noted that private and illegal networks had contributed to the dissemination of dual-use technologies and that the threat to European citizens from WMD proliferation had grown in the five years since the WMD Strategy was adopted. If these weapons found their way into the hands of certain states or terrorists, the 'New Lines' warned, it would constitute 'one of the greatest security challenges which Europeans may ever face'.[8] The Report on the Implementation of the ESS, released in the same month, agreed that the risk had increased and had put the multilateral framework under pressure,[9] an implicit recognition that non-proliferation efforts thus far had been insufficient to meet the challenge.

The EU's strategy against WMD proliferation

The WMD Strategy laid out a multi-layered strategy against WMD proliferation in some detail. Its major principles are 'effective multilateralism', promotion of a stable regional and international environment, close cooperation with partners, and strengthening EU structures. The strategy underlined the need to integrate the wide range of available instruments, which included multilateral treaties and verification mechanisms, national and internationally coordinated export controls, cooperative threat-reduction programmes, political and economic levers (including trade and development policies), interdiction of illegal procurement activities, and coercive measures in accordance with the UN Charter as a last resort. The strategy stressed that while all of these instruments are necessary, none is sufficient in itself.[10] Some of these principles and instruments are outlined below, along with newer initiatives promulgated since 2003 to support the strategy, including numerous Joint Actions and the 'New Lines'.

'Effective multilateralism'

The ESS's emphasis on an effective multilateral system for security was reflected in the WMD Strategy, which argued that 'effective multilateralism is the cornerstone of the European strategy for combating proliferation of WMD'.[11] The focus on effective multilateralism is to a great extent a reaction to the unilateralism and disregard for international organisations that many felt characterised US leadership under G.W. Bush. Yet the EU describes the transatlantic relationship as 'irreplaceable' and stresses the importance of cooperation with the US, along with other 'key partners' such as Japan, Canada, Russia and UN organisations. The specific components of the 'European' multilateral approach include pledges to pursue the universalisation and strengthening of major non-proliferation treaties and agreements, to reinforce compliance with the multilateral treaty regime, to provide political, financial and technical support to verification regimes to ensure effective detection and deter non-compliance, to strengthen export controls, to enhance the security of proliferation-sensitive materials, equipment and expertise in the EU, and to harmonise anti-trafficking regimes.

The strategy acknowledged the importance of the Nuclear Non-Proliferation Treaty (NPT), the International Atomic Energy Agency (IAEA)'s safeguard agreements and the Additional Protocol, the Chemical Weapons Convention (CWC), the Biological and Toxin Weapons Convention (BTWC), and the entry into force of the Comprehensive Test-Ban Treaty (CTBT). It also expressed the EU's hopes for the introduction of an international Fissile Material Cut-Off Treaty (FMCT) and pledged to assist other countries to fulfil their treaty and regime obligations.

The strategy conceded that the non-proliferation regime's credibility depended upon the enforcement of its rules by the broader international community – an argument used by many proponents of the Iraq War. Indeed, the WMD Strategy allows that, if preventative measures have failed, coercive measures (including the use of force) can be envisioned. Yet the strategy emphasises the importance of strengthening the role of the UN Security Council as the 'final arbiter' on the consequences for states of non-compliance – a particularly contentious issue at the time of its publication given the divisions of the Security Council on the legitimate use of force before the Iraq War.

In its promise to support verification regimes, the strategy again stresses the importance of existing mechanisms and organisations. This support includes diplomatic efforts to encourage countries to ratify the IAEA Additional Protocol, following the example of all EU member states; supporting organisations such as the IAEA, CTBT Organisation and the Organisation for the Prohibition of Chemical Weapons (OPCW); and assisting conventions such as the BTWC to develop the verification mechanism that it lacked. (In 2001 the US had blocked attempts to introduce a verification protocol, a position that the Obama administration had not reversed at the time of writing). The Security Council has since adopted numerous Joint Actions under the Common Foreign and Security Policy supporting international organisations relevant to non-proliferation, such as the IAEA, the OPCW, the CTBTO, the BTWC and the World Health Organisation.[12]

The strategy emphasised the importance of encouraging new states to join the various export control regimes and, in addition, to improve export controls within an expanded EU through enhanced information sharing and coordination of EU positions, as well as strengthening the regimes themselves. The ten states acceding to EU membership just months after the publication of the WMD Strategy provided an immediate test of these goals. Peer reviews across Europe have been conducted in order to improve best practice across the EU.[13] European industries have a long history of being targeted by proliferating states (such as Iraq, Iran or Pakistan) or proliferation networks (such as the A.Q. Khan network) for the combination of their high-quality products and, particularly before the First Gulf War, their often-weak export control systems.[14] Strengthening both their own, and other states', export controls is therefore a crucial way of contributing to improved non-proliferation standards.

UN Security Council Resolution 1540 was passed in 2004, calling on all states to refrain from supporting non-state actors in the proliferation of nuclear, chemical and biological weapons and their means of delivery; and to adopt and enforce appropriate laws to prevent them from doing so. Although it was adopted under Chapter VII of UN Charter, making it legally binding on all states, it lacks a verification mechanism and has been implemented very unevenly. Many states have failed to fulfil their reporting requirements and have been unable or unwilling to enact the necessary internal reforms to comply with its instructions on ensuring that they did not provide support for non-state actors in the proliferation of WMD. The Security Council adopted Joint Actions in support of UN 1540 in 2006 and 2008, aimed at raising awareness of national requirements under UNSCR 1540 and assisting third countries (the EU's term for non-EU states) to build capacity to implement the resolution.[15] In 2008 the 'New Lines' called for intensified cooperation with third countries to improve their export controls.

Recognising the importance of strengthening the security of chemical, biological, radiological and nuclear materials within the EU, in 2009 the European Commission issued an EU CBRN Action Plan, with estimated budgetary support of up to €100 million between 2010 and 2013 (drawn from existing programmes).[16]

The WMD Strategy called on member states to adopt common policies related to the criminal punishment for exporting, brokering and smuggling WMD-related material, as well as considering measures against the transit, transhipment of sensitive materials and possibly the interception of illegal shipments. The EU and its member states are fully committed to the US-led Proliferation Security Initiative (PSI), under which countries interdict cargo that is suspected of carrying WMD-related materials.[17]

Promoting a stable international and regional environment
The EU hopes to tackle the 'demand-side' of proliferation: its position underlined in the WMD Strategy is that 'the best solution to the problem of proliferation of WMD is that countries should no longer feel they need them ... The more secure coun-

tries feel, the more likely they are to abandon programmes'. The strategy highlights the important role that can be played by positive and negative security assurances. However, the EU is clear-eyed about the possibility of resolving all the political 'root causes' of proliferation in the short term, underlining that its policy is 'to prevent, deter, halt and, where possible, eliminate proliferation programmes of concern, while dealing with their underlying causes'.[18]

While the WMD Strategy made few direct references to promoting international disarmament, in recent years the EU has mirrored the Obama administration's policy of treating disarmament measures seriously. In a speech to the European Parliament in December 2008, Solana argued that there was a perception, particularly in the developing world, of an imbalance between the three so-called pillars of the non-proliferation regime (non-proliferation, 'peaceful use' of nuclear technology and disarmament). He argued that it was 'in our common interest to address this trust deficit'.[19] In addition to supporting the 'peaceful use' element through measures such as pledging €25m to the IAEA's nuclear fuel bank proposal, the EU has placed enhanced rhetorical emphasis on the need to take meaningful disarmament measures. Like the Obama administration, the EU feels that this policy serves to reduce pressure on the NPT by diminishing the charges of double standards levelled at nuclear-weapon states by non-aligned countries, and also makes non-nuclear-weapon states feel more secure and hence less likely to proliferate themselves.

There is an inherent tension in formulating a coherent EU policy on nuclear disarmament, given the membership of two nuclear-weapon states within the EU[20] and the overlap of the Union's membership with that of NATO. Of the two EU nuclear-weapon states, France in particular has been more reluctant to embrace near-term disarmament measures.[21] Yet both France and the UK have in principle accepted measures towards longer-term disarmament, and have made reductions to their nuclear arsenals in recent years.

Despite differences between member states, the EU has been able to formulate Common Positions for NPT Review Conferences. In 2010 this was delivered by Baroness Ashton, the recently appointed EU High Representative for foreign and security policy. Although the language in this statement was perhaps more restrained than that hoped for by some EU non-nuclear-weapon states, it underlined the EU's belief that the 'three pillars' were mutually reinforcing, and reaffirmed the EU's commitment to 'creating the conditions for a world without nuclear weapons'.[22] Importantly, the EU conviction that 'intermediate steps on our path towards this objective can also represent significant increases in security for all' had earlier appeared in an EU–US Declaration on Non-proliferation and Disarmament in November 2009.[23] Yet, as with its policy of improving regional security so as to reduce the 'demand-side' of proliferation, the careful wording of the EU's language about disarmament suggests that, like the Obama administration, it is aware that disarmament is at best a long-term goal, and that measures to promote it should strengthen the non-proliferation agenda, not replace it.

To mitigate the risk of WMD terrorism originating from abroad, European threat-reduction programmes have been expanded, funded both through national contributions and through EU budgets. The EU has engaged in threat reduction activities since 1999,[24] but it has stepped up its involvement in this field in recent years, with a particular focus on scientist redirection, export controls on dual-use goods, and illicit trafficking of nuclear materials. The geographical scope of EU assistance is spreading from the former Soviet Union to new regions such as Southeast Asia, the Middle East and Africa.[25] The EU has funded a variety of these threat-reduction programmes under the Instrument for Stability (IfS) and the Instrument for Nuclear Safety Cooperation (INSC), with the Joint Research Centre (JRC), the scientific and technical arm of the Commission, also involved. Approximately €123 million has been devoted to CBRN risk-mitigation projects under the IfS programme for 2009–11.[26] One IfS initiative to establish a network of CBRN centres of excellence, the first stage of which was launched in 2009,[27] could create an effective mechanism for the dissemination of best practice, assuming that the EU does not duplicate the work of member states.[28] All EU member states are now 'partner nations' of the Global Initiative to Combat Nuclear Terrorism, and the EU itself enjoys observer status within the Initiative.[29] The EU is also now the largest contributor to the International Atomic Energy Agency's Nuclear Security Fund, with its support expected to exceed €30m by the end of 2010.[30] The EU is a member of the G8 Global Partnership Against the Spread of Weapons and Materials of Mass Destruction, and committed itself to spend €1 billion of EU funds over and above pledges by EU member states in the ten years from 2002. Although the EU had committed €955m it had only spent some €635m of this by 2010.[31] This can largely be attributed to bureaucratic obstructions in partner states receiving assistance, although EU accounting requirements have also contributed to the under-spend.[32]

As advocated in the WMD Strategy, the EU has also sought to bring proliferation issues into the mainstream by integrating non-proliferation policy into its political and economic agreements with third countries. Based on the precedent of the 'human rights clause' introduced into agreements with third countries in the 1990s, a non-proliferation clause was adopted by the Council in November 2003, and was intended to be included in agreements with third countries so that cooperation would be conditional on satisfactory non-proliferation behaviour. In theory, this instrument could allow the EU to harness its commercial strength in the service of non-proliferation goals. However, the effectiveness of the clause has been called into question. Although the EU has concluded negotiations for agreements that would include a WMD clause with nearly 100 countries, only two had entered into force by 2009. The EU has been inconsistent in its application of the clause; for example, during negotiations for a free-trade agreement India resisted any efforts to influence its arms-control policies through inclusion of the clause. Few criteria exist to establish whether a state has fallen below the requisite non-proliferation standards; and the EU need only include a requirement within the WMD clause that countries fulfil existing non-proliferation obligations, not that they take on additional ones. [33] In the 'New Lines' of 2008, the Council called for an assessment of the implementation of the WMD clause in order to examine ways to improve negotiations on the clause, evaluate its implementation, and explore how to trigger the clause in the case of non-compliance.[34] Although the Council published a short document in 2009 on the implementation of the WMD clause, this did not contain the assessments called for in the 'New Lines'.[35]

Developing EU structures and improving coordination

The WMD Strategy recommended a six-monthly review of its implementation.[36] It also recommended establishing a 'WMD monitoring centre' to oversee the consistent implementation of the Strategy and the collection of information and intelligence in liaison with the EU's intelligence analysis agency, the EU Situation Centre. However, a second written recommendation, from the personal representative on nonproliferation of WMD in 2006, served merely to highlight delays in setting up the monitoring centre.[37] When it eventually took shape, it proved to be a far less dynamic structure than some may have originally hoped for. The June 2010 WMD Strategy Progress Report suggested the newly created body resembled more a coordination mechanism, chaired by the EU representative on non-proliferation and disarmament, than a physical establishment or institution. In the first half of 2010, only two meetings of the centre took place.

In 2005 a UK parliamentary report identified divided responsibilities and insufficient resources within the EU as possible obstacles to the adequate implementation of the WMD Strategy, arguing that, while the Council bore responsibility for the strategy, most resources and instruments were controlled by the Commission. It expressed concern at suggestions that 'turf wars' may have impeded the flow of information between the Council Secretariat and the Commission, and warned that individuals within the Council Secretariat and Commission may not have received adequate financial or administrative support.[38]

The EU appears to be aware of problems in coordinating both its own institutions and the policies of member states. In 2008 the 'Updated List of Priorities for the implementation of the EU WMD Strategy' and the 'New Lines' set goals for raising the profile of nonproliferation measures within the EU and turning non-proliferation into a 'cross-cutting priority' of EU and member states' policies;[39] encouraging better coordination and 'optimal mobilisation' of member states' policies;[40] and improving the EU's efficiency in the field of non-proliferation through improved internal coordination, particularly by reinforcing the role of the WMD Centre through 'regular participation of all relevant Council and Commission services and member states'.[41] These suggest that the EU has continued to experience difficulties in coordinating the various institutions and instruments involved in implementing its WMD

Strategy. In an interview in February 2009, a senior EU official acknowledged that the 'New Lines' were mainly intended to improve coherence among EU states.[42] At the time of writing, it is still unclear what effect the Lisbon Treaty, including the new European External Action Service, may have on the EU's ability to implement its WMD strategy in a more coherent fashion.

Non-proliferation in practice: the EU and Iran

Although much of the WMD Strategy's emphasis is on preventative and cooperation action, its avowed objective is to 'prevent, deter, *halt* and, where possible, *eliminate* proliferation programmes of concern worldwide' [emphasis added], and thus includes the possibility of coercive disarmament diplomacy. While noting that the first line of defence is to employ political and diplomatic preventative measures (such as multilateral treaties and export-control regimes) and work through international organisations, the strategy acknowledges that if these should fail, coercive measures under Chapter VII of the UN Charter and international law, such as sanctions, interception of shipments and the use of force, as appropriate, should be envisioned, with the UN Security Council playing a central role.

The most significant WMD proliferation challenge facing the EU is the threat that Iran will acquire a nuclear-weapons capability, if not an actual nuclear arsenal. The current Iranian nuclear crisis emerged in 2002–03, in the same period that the United States was leading a campaign to disarm Iraq by force. However, at least in their early stages, efforts to prevent Iran developing a nuclear-weapons capability were directed by European states and the EU itself. As an example of the EU's strategy in action against a non-proliferation 'hard case', it warrants closer examination.

The threat from Iran's nuclear activities[43]

In 2002–03 it became clear that Iran had been engaged in numerous activities relating to fissile-material production since the mid-1980s. Contrary to its safeguards agreements, these had not been disclosed to the IAEA. In 2003, the United Kingdom, France and Germany (known as the 'E3') initiated a diplomatic effort to restore confidence in Iran's intentions. A year later the EU High Representative for the CFSP joined the negotiations. During the course of these negotiations Iran partially and inter-mittently suspended its enrichment programme. However, after rejecting a proposal by the E3 for a 'Framework for a Long-term Agreement', Iran resumed uranium-conversion activities in August 2005. It was found to be in non-compliance with its safeguards obligations in September 2005. Iran resumed uranium enrichment in January 2006, and was then referred to the United Nations Security Council.

In June 2006 and again in June 2008, the E3, together with Russia, China and the United States (collectively known as the E3+3) made diplomatic proposals that were presented to Iran by the EU high representative. These contained multiple incentives that the E3+3 would be willing to negotiate with Iran once it had suspended its enrichment-related and reprocess-ing activities. Numerous Security Council resolutions issued between August 2006 and June 2010 calling on Iran to suspend these activities have been ignored.[44] Since 2006 Iran has also refused to ratify or implement the Additional Protocol which it had signed in 2003. This, along with its lack of cooperation with the IAEA's investigation into past suspicious activity, left the agency unable to 'provide credible assurance about the absence of undeclared nuclear material and activities in Iran'.[45] The exposure in September 2009 of a previously-undisclosed enrichment plant near Qom confirmed suspicions that Iran had established clandestine facilities that were almost certainly intended to contribute to a nuclear-weapons capability. Hopes were briefly raised in the autumn of 2009 that a fuel-swap deal could be enacted in which Iran would export the bulk of its low-enriched uranium (LEU) stockpile, in return for fuel assemblies of 19.75% enriched uranium that would be used to refuel its Tehran Research Reactor. However, Iran eventually rejected the conditions of the deal as they were originally agreed, and has resubmitted proposals for an agreement under unacceptable parameters that would largely negate the security and confidence-building goals of the original deal.[46]

Since the crisis began, Iran has maintained that its nuclear activities are entirely peaceful and that it merely intends to use nuclear energy for electricity generation, as is its right under Article IV of the NPT. Even without taking into account the pattern of deception displayed over almost 20 years in concealing its activities, the multiple military connections to the nuclear programme[47] and Iran's contact with the A.Q. Khan proliferation network, this explanation is deeply unconvincing. At the core of the Iranian nuclear issue is Iran's desire to produce fissile material using dual-use technology, not its pursuit of peaceful nuclear energy, which is endorsed by all of the E3+3 states as well as the EU. Iran has refused multiple offers of extensive assistance for its development of nuclear energy, including the possible sale of light-water power reactors, nuclear fuel assurances and/or participation in multinational fuel consortia, if these would entail forgoing enrichment on its own soil and the nuclear-weapons capability this would impart. Although its justification is that it cannot depend on external suppliers, Iran possesses insufficient uranium reserves to be self-reliant in nuclear fuel for power reactors, so independence from international fuel markets would never be feasible. In addition, the sole Iranian power reactor near completion, at Bushehr, can only be operated with fuel assemblies supplied by Russia and possibly the US-based nuclear engineering firm Westinghouse. Yet Iran persists in developing its enrichment capabilities despite their immense diplomatic and economic costs. The EU has likened this situation to trying to produce gasoline without having a car.[48] Similarly, Iran's February 2010 decision to begin enriching uranium to 20% (supposedly to be eventually fabricated into fuel for the Tehran Research Reactor) is difficult to attribute to peaceful intentions, given the country's inability to fabricate indigenously the specific fuel elements that are required to operate this reactor. The most logical explanation for Iran's behaviour is that it is determined to possess a nuclear-weapons capability, if not a nuclear weapon itself.

As of September 2010, Iran had approximately 8,800 centrifuges installed at its main plant at Natanz, of which around 3,700 were producing LEU.[49] Iran had accumulated a stockpile of around 2,800kg of LEU, sufficient for two weapons if the material could be further enriched to weapons-grade uranium. Iran's enrichment programme has suffered from technical setbacks since 2009, some of which may be attributable to foreign interference.[50] Despite this, it is likely that, if it were to make the political decision to do so, Iran would be technically capable of producing weapons-grade uranium, constructing nuclear weapons and developing the missiles to deliver them to targets as far away as Western Europe within approximately five to ten years.[51] It is also conceivable that Iran could threaten European cities earlier than this using terrorist proxies, because a simple nuclear device, deliverable by truck or ship or constructed in place, would not require the development of long-range ballistic missiles or complex weaponisation procedures. However, although it is highly likely that Iran's leaders desire the technical capability to produce a nuclear weapon, it is less certain whether they have made the decision to actually pursue this in the near future, let alone to use one offensively.[52]

Some analysts have argued that Iran could be content with merely a 'break-out capability': the ability to break out of the NPT and produce nuclear weapons within a short period. In addition, even if Iran were to acquire actual nuclear weapons, it could probably be successfully deterred from using them, as was Stalin's USSR and Mao's China.[53] By contrast, others have argued that Iran not only wishes to obtain nuclear weapons but, due to the regime's revolutionary ideology, and the apocalyptic worldview of President Mahmoud Ahmadinejad and some of his supporters that derives from the martyr culture of 'Twelver' Shiism to which they adhere, a nuclear Iran would not only be undeterrable, it may actually perceive mutually assured destruction as an inducement.[54] This argument is less persuasive. The prospect of Iran developing nuclear weapons is uncertain, and the probability that it would intentionally use them or transfer them to terrorist proxies is much smaller. However, this cannot be discounted entirely and, given the catastrophic consequences of nuclear use, this scenario deserves to be taken seriously.

Unintentional use

If Iran developed nuclear weapons then, even assuming that it has no desire to use them on its adversaries, their very existence would create the possibility of unintentional nuclear use in the Middle East. Although the mutual nuclear deterrence between the US and USSR during the Cold War appeared to be stable (and indeed a stabilising influence in international relations), there were several occasions (particularly during the earlier periods of their deterrent relationship) when both sides came close to miscalculation, most notably the Cuban Missile Crisis of 1962. This was despite the fact that the US and Soviet Union had full diplomatic relations and essentially had to manage a deterrent relationship with only one other actor. Iran has no diplomatic relations with Israel, its most obvious nuclear antagonist, and it is easy to imagine a scenario in the context of an immature deterrent relationship in which conventional conflict could escalate swiftly, particularly if Iranian nuclear command and control systems were weak. In addition (as described in greater detail below), it is likely that Iran's neighbours would seek to mirror its nuclear deterrent. A poly-nuclear Middle East would greatly decrease the chances of maintaining stable deterrence. Finally, an increase in the number of nuclear weapons, particularly in states with little experience in nuclear security and safety, raises the likelihood of accidents or theft.

Indirect threats

Given its fractious nature and uncertain future, it is difficult to predict the intentions of the Iranian regime. From the perspective of the EU, however, it is evident that an Iranian nuclear capability in itself presents threats aside from the starker, albeit unlikely, scenario of intentional nuclear use by the Islamic Republic. Although it is impossible to analyse these less direct threats comprehensively here, some of them are outlined below. These threats would be posed by a non-weaponised Iranian nuclear capability; if Iran acquired an actual nuclear weapon, their severity would be exacerbated.

A regional proliferation cascade with global implications

In 2003 the ESS noted the possibility of a WMD arms race, 'particularly in the Middle East'. In March 2010 the high representative for foreign affairs and security policy stated in Cairo that '[the EU's] position is based on a firm belief that an Iran with nuclear weapons risks triggering a proliferation cascade throughout the Middle East. This is the last thing this region needs. A nuclear weapons free Middle East remains a European goal.'[55]

Since 2006, most countries in the Middle East have announced new or revived plans to explore civilian nuclear energy. It is likely that at least part of their motivation stems from concern at Iran's nuclear development. Some, such as Turkey and Egypt, have specifically refused to exclude the possibility of developing sensitive enrichment and reprocessing technologies. If Iran's pursuit of a nuclear-weapons capability continues, it is possible that other regional states will seek a deterrent capability of their own.[56] This would increase regional instability and greatly magnify the stakes of potential conflicts.

In the broader global context, Iran's successful defiance of multiple Security Council resolutions that had judged its nuclear programme to be illegal would deal the international non-proliferation regime a severe blow. Iran's acquisition of a nuclear-weapon capability, possibly then mirrored by its Middle Eastern neighbours, could intensify existing proliferation drivers in other regions such as Northeast Asia. If Iran's activities promoted the perception that the non-proliferation regime was unenforceable and gradually eroding, many other states could decide that their own security would be best served by pursuing nuclear capabilities. This dynamic could lead to the collapse of the non-proliferation regime, quashing hopes of working towards a world free of nuclear weapons.

Unintentional transfer of nuclear technology or materials

Regardless of whether the regime would deliberately choose to transfer nuclear weapons or fissile material to terrorist proxies, an Iranian nuclear-weapons capability increases the probability that nuclear technologies and/or materials would spread elsewhere. The A.Q. Khan proliferation network emerged from Khan's illicit procurement activities for the Pakistani nuclear programme. Given the connections with technology suppliers that the Iranian Revolutionary Guard Corps (IRGC) must have forged as a result of its dominant role in Iran's clandestine nuclear procurement, it is possible that elements within the IRGC could transfer or sell nuclear technology or materials to non-state actors or other countries.[57] Such transactions could be driven by financial gain or religious motivations, and would not necessarily be authorised or performed with official knowledge.

This threat would be magnified if other regional states pursue their own nuclear programmes in response to Iran, as described above. As more nuclear material and technology is introduced into the Middle East, a region that is highly susceptible to terrorism, religious radicalism and political instability, the chances of this material and technology being stolen or diverted increase, unless stringent nuclear security measures are applied.

A more coercive Iran

If it were believed that Iran possessed a nuclear capability; that is, it was thought to be 'one turn of the screwdriver away' from an actual bomb, it may well feel a sense of invulnerability from conventional military attack. This could in turn encourage it to assume a more assertive, and possibly aggressive attitude towards its neighbours in the Gulf and/or Israel. This could lead to increased interference by Iran using its proxies in Afghanistan against European forces and possibly within Europe itself. In addition, if diplomatic or economic methods to halt Iran's development of nuclear capabilities appear ineffective, the probability of Israel and/or the United States taking military action against the nuclear programme would increase.

The Gulf Arab states are keenly aware of past Iranian territorial encroachments (such as seizing the Abu Musa and Tunbs islands); and Iran's desire for regional dominance predates the revolutionary era. The Middle East is the source of a significant portion of the EU's oil imports, so any coercive behaviour by Iran against its neighbours, or actual conflict in the Gulf or the broader Middle East, could pose a threat to European energy security.

The next conflict between Israel and Hizbullah or Hamas (both widely perceived in Israel as Iranian proxies) could operate under different dynamics from either the 2006 Lebanon War or the 2008 *Operation Cast Lead* in Gaza, if their enemies' main sponsor were nuclear capable. In such a conflict, Hizbullah or Hamas may not be deterred from attacking Israeli strategic assets such as Tel Aviv or Ben Gurion airport, which could in turn lead to a severe escalation.

The EU has designated the resolution of the Arab–Israeli conflict a strategic priority.[58] Iran has demonstrated its hostility towards the Middle East peace process, and its acquisition of a nuclear capability would do little to strengthen prospects of a comprehensive resolution. Instead, it is likely that this would bolster radical elements opposed to any workable solution. There is strong evidence that Iran has provided heavy weapons and explosives to the Taliban and other militants in Afghanistan.[59] It is not inconceivable that the sense of impunity bestowed by an Iranian nuclear capability would give it greater licence to target European armed forces in Afghanistan, or those serving in UNIFIL, the UN mission in Lebanon, if EU–Iran relations deteriorated or in the event of a US–Israeli attack against Iran's nuclear programme.

Iran has previously sponsored terrorism against European interests. In 1983 Hizbullah killed 58 French paratroopers in Beirut, and was involved in the bombing of the French Embassy in Kuwait in the same year, as well as in numerous attacks in France in 1986.[60] Iran issued a fatwa calling for the death of British author Salman Rushdie in 1989, after elements of his novel *The Satanic Verses* were condemned as blasphemous by Muslim clerics. A 2006 British government report warned of the possibility of 'an increased threat to UK interests from Iranian state-sponsored terrorism should the diplomatic situation [concerning the nuclear programme] deteriorate'.[61] The UK's envoy to the UN Sir John Sawers, who has since been appointed chief of the UK Secret Intelligence Service, reported in February 2009 that Iran made an explicit offer to kill fewer British servicemen through its proxies in Iraq in return for a more lenient UK policy towards its nuclear programme.[62]

Although not a direct threat to European security, it is probable that the Iranian regime, were it emboldened by the possession of a nuclear capability and the awareness that international intervention could not take place on humanitarian grounds, would feel confident enough to suppress internal dissent with greater brutality, leading to an increase in human-rights abuses.

An effective EU strategy?

Since 2003 the E3 and, from 2004, the EU itself, have been at the forefront of diplomacy surrounding the Iranian nuclear problem.[63] From 2003 until 2005, the E3's diplomacy appeared to yield some positive results, such as the Tehran Agreement in 2003 and the Brussels and Paris Agreements of 2004. Iran signed the Additional Protocol, and at times appeared willing to suspend enrichment-related activities, although it never agreed to a permanent cessation. However, since 2005, Iran has adopted a more intransigent policy, resuming its nuclear activities and rejecting the numerous diplomatic overtures made to it. The E3 and EU have taken a dual-track approach: backing UN resolutions and sanctions against Iran, while repeating that they were willing to resume negotiations once Iran against suspended its nuclear activities. The high representative for the Common Foreign and Security Policy effectively served as the main interlocutor with Iran during much of this period, delivering both the June 2006 and June 2008 E3+3 proposals to Iran. The E3 and EU have generally maintained unity in their policy goals, although there have been occasional reports of disagreements within either the EU or the E3 on diplomatic strategy.[64]

If Iran is to be peacefully persuaded to change course, the perceived advantages of a nuclear capability will need to be offset through a compelling combination of incentives and disincentives. The EU has made clear that it is willing to engage with Iran, not only in an attempt to resolve the nuclear issue, but also to improve relations more broadly. Iran has rejected these attempts at substantive dialogue and refused to suspend its nuclear activities, even temporarily. Indeed, in July 2009 Iran declared that the alleged interference of the EU in its presidential elections had left the EU 'unqualified' to hold further talks about the nuclear programme. A year later, Iran's lead nuclear negotiator dismissed as 'astonishing' an offer from Baroness Ashton to resume talks after the passage of the June 2010 UN sanctions resolution.[65] Although, at the time of writing, Iran has indicated that it is willing to re-enter negotiations with the E3+3, it has refused to confirm a possible timeframe for such talks several times, and there are few indications thus far that it is willing to make concessions on its nuclear activities. Iran has demonstrated that the incentives offered by the E3+3 are insufficient to persuade it to change its nuclear policy, and has dismissed any restrictions on its nuclear programme that would prevent a future weapons capability. The Iranian regime appears to discount the probability of an American or Israeli military attack that would threaten its survival and has given few indications that it seeks security assurances from the US, let alone the EU. If there are indeed incentives sufficiently enticing to persuade Iran to abandon its nuclear programme, it seems unlikely that these could be provided by the EU.

If the EU wishes to maintain a role as a credible actor in the Iranian nuclear problem, it must play to its strengths and exploit the leverage it may have over Iranian decision-making. This lies in its dominant economic relationship with Iran: the EU is Iran's largest trading partner.[66] In 2009, however, Iran ranked only 26th on the list of sources of EU imports (0.7% of the total) and 25th in terms of EU exports (0.9% of total exports). Conversely, European imports play a crucial role in Iranian industry. A former president of the German–Iranian Chamber of Industry and Commerce in Tehran has stated that approximately two-thirds of Iranian industry relies on German engineering products (even though in 2008 Iran was only Germany's 42nd-largest export destination, with the €3.92bn of sales comprising only 0.4% of all German exports). In 2009, machinery comprised 40% of all European exports to Iran. European technology provides an indispensable contribution to Iran's petrochemical sector, which in turn comprises the vast majority of Iranian exports. This sector will require substantial modernisation in coming years if it is to maintain its current levels of production, already diminished from its peak in the 1970s.[67]

The E3 introduced the draft resolution that was to become UNSCR 1737 in December 2006 (the first resolution to apply sanctions to Iran) and the UK and France have played leading roles in support of the other Security Council resolutions. These resolutions have mandated various sanctions or other restrictive measures aimed at persuading Iran to return to negotiations. The EU has not only implemented these UN resolutions, but has also broadened their scope by extending travel bans to additional individuals, enacting a more comprehensive arms embargo, and freezing the assets of individuals and entities beyond those specified by the UN. In 2008 the EU froze the assets of several entities, including Iran's largest bank, and authorised member states to increase checks on ships or aircraft destined for Iran if they were suspected of transporting banned goods. Many European firms, under increasing pressure from the US, have divested from, stopped potential new investments in, and/or ended dollar transactions with Iran. These include BP, Siemens and Total. In 2008 the US Treasury and State Departments announced that they had persuaded more than 40 banks, including HSBC, Deutsche Bank and UBS, not to provide financing for exports to Iran nor to process dollar transactions for Iranian banks.[68] Negotiations for a Trade and Cooperation Agreement (TCA) have been suspended since Iran's resumption of its nuclear activities in 2005. The EU has ensured that its lists of Iranian individuals and entities subject to freezing measures and dual-use items prohibited from export to Iran are kept updated.[69]

In July 2010 the EU imposed a new range of sanctions against Iran that went beyond the measures mandated by UNSCR 1929 the previous month. These sanctions target Iran's energy, transport, banking and insurance sectors. Notably, they ban any new European investment in Iran's petrochemical industry, including the sale of equipment for use in oil and gas exploration, refining activity or the production of liquid natural gas. Although certain EU member states, most notably Sweden, voiced concerns about these stringent new sanctions, the EU succeeded in reaching consensus among its 27 members.[70] The EU is to be commended for acting as one on meaningful measures that will actually have a detrimental effect on European commerce. The revelations of the Qom enrichment plant, Iran's prevarications over the proposed fuel-swap deal and the decision to enrich uranium to 20% contributed to the EU's sense of resolve.

Concerted efforts by the EU could contribute to severe pressure on the Iranian economy,[71] perhaps sufficient to alter the regime's nuclear calculus. Although sanctions may not succeed, their effectiveness will certainly be diminished if EU member states discount their potential from the outset, and so vigorous efforts should be made to ensure that the sanctions are applied consistently. Conversely, if Iran is convinced of Europe's determination to enforce these measures, then their deterrent effect will be greatly enhanced and the necessity of imposing them for a prolonged period will be reduced. Some EU member states may feel that they are being asked to bear a disproportionate economic cost of imposing strict sanctions against Iran. They will need to be convinced that the consequences of a nuclear Iran, a poly-nuclear Middle East, and the potential collapse of the global non-proliferation regime outweigh short-term economic advantages.

It is true that strict, targeted sanctions may well not succeed in dissuading Iran. Yet the alternatives (acquiescence in an Iranian nuclear-weapon capability or military action against the programme) are far more disadvantageous. Moreover, Iran should not be allowed to acquire a nuclear-weapon capability without paying a severe penalty; if it were to do so, its calculation that the benefits of manipulating the NPT outweighed the costs will have been publicly validated. This could encourage other states to follow its example.

Conclusions

The EU can play a vital role in bolstering the international non-proliferation regime by strengthening and universalising its treaties, conventions and the other component parts of its international architecture. In practical terms, the EU can also make a powerful contribution through the promotion of best practices, both within the EU itself and also with third countries. The promotion of strong measures in nuclear, radiological, chemical and biological security will be particularly important in the context of a global expansion in nuclear power, growing industrial sectors in the developing world, and the spread of biotechnology. In addition, the effect of 27 European states acting in concert contributes to a normative trend in favour of the non-proliferation regime. In these senses, Europe's role as a 'good non-proliferation citizen' is a crucial one.

Holding Iran to account for its violations of both the letter and spirit of its non-proliferation obligations and exacting a price for its continued non-compliance can be seen as another way of strengthening the non-proliferation architecture. If these efforts fail, there will certainly be serious consequences for the non-proliferation regime, in addition to the other grave threats posed to European security by an Iranian nuclear-weapons capability.

European states, and the EU itself, were eager for the Iranian nuclear problem to be the first high-profile success of Europe's non-proliferation strategy, to restore confidence in multilateralism following the divisions prior to the Iraq War and to stand in contrast to the growing fiasco emerging in the aftermath of the American-led occupation. Yet although European states have broadly maintained a consensus in their dealings with Iran, it should be remembered that the diplomatic process is a means to resolve the Iranian nuclear problem, not an end in itself. Although the EU finally seems prepared to adopt stringent coercive measures, it remains to be seen whether it is now too late for such measures to be effective enough to dissuade Iran from its current course. Iran's acquisition of a nuclear-weapon capability, despite the better part of a decade of European diplomacy, would ultimately represent a failure of the EU's WMD proliferation strategy, and undermine the EU's reputation as an effective actor on the world stage.

CHAPTER EIGHT

Energy Security

Virginia Comolli
Research Analyst, IISS

The term 'energy security' is subject to differing interpretations from economists and foreign-policy analysts. For the former the concept itself is flawed: energy supplies should be regarded as a matter determined exclusively by market dynamics rather than relations between countries. The latter maintain that energy is a security matter as it relates to the politics of energy and resource management.

It can be argued that a country is *energy secure* when energy is available at a reasonable price and access to resources is uninterrupted, but contrasting views exist with regard to what should be protected and from what risks. Arguments vary from protection against terrorist attacks and coping with price shocks, to politically induced interruptions of energy supply and technical failure. For others it means addressing the effects of global warming.[1] The relation between energy security and climate change is in itself rather controversial; a number of experts see the two as closely intertwined, as climate concerns have an impact on energy choices and related costs. In particular, the increasing demands for energy forces decision-makers to balance this need against the consequences of dependence on fossil fuels. A more environmentally friendly alternative would be to invest in nuclear power, but this option carries its own security concerns.[2] Other experts deny the climate–energy link and prefer to address energy issues separately. Viewed from either perspective, European countries are facing considerable risks with regard to energy, not the least of which are price hikes, resource exhaustion and the politicisation of energy.

Risks for Europe

Price shocks

All commodities, including energy resources and oil in particular, are subject to major price swings over time. Presenting the European Commission's latest Strategic Energy Review in November 2008, José Manuel Barroso said: 'Energy prices have risen by an average of 15% in the European Union in the last year. 54% of Europe's energy is imported at a cost of 700 euro for every EU citizen'.[3] Figure 1 shows how the price of oil has been subject to a 200% increase from January 2000 to July 2010, experiencing fluctuations between $17.5 (November 2001) and $145.31 (July 2008).

These changes are linked to the overall business cycle, rising and decreasing demand and geopolitical issues. The summer 2008 price rise – a product of an imbalance between demand and ability to supply – raised the question of whether it was still feasible to rely on fossil fuel. Indeed, many wondered whether the end of the oil era was eventually approaching.[4] Drastic increases create imbalances between producing countries and consumers and put the latter's economies at risk. Energy price drops also bring negative economic consequences as they 'tend to diminish the capacity-enhancing investment in energy producing countries, creating new bottlenecks in oil and gas supply'.[5] Also, economic regulations imposed by the governments of producing countries might influence the level

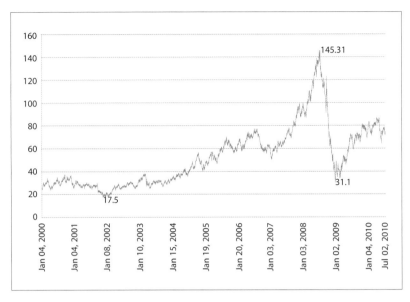

Figure 1: **Oil price (dollars per barrel)** (Energy Information Administration)

of investments, which would then have an effect on prices and production.

Resource exhaustion

Although BP's annual statistical review points out that as a result of the global financial recession 'world primary energy consumption – including oil, natural gas, coal, nuclear and hydro power – fell by 1.1% in 2009, the first decline since 1982 and the largest decline (in percentage terms) since 1980',[6] in the EU both gas and oil reserves continue to diminish. Oil production, for instance, has witnessed a 6.1% reduction between 2008 and 2009.[7] This trend is made even more worrisome by the fact that access to reserves outside the EU borders is not always easy, as more than 90% of hydrocarbon reserves are to be found in volatile areas in Eurasia and the Middle East.[8] Looking at oil, recent estimates place the world's proven reserves at 1–1.2 trillion barrels. Some extra 700 billion barrels are deemed feasible to be extracted by the US Geological Survey and it has been calculated that a further trillion barrels can be extracted, bringing the total up to 3tr barrels. At current consumption rates, this total reserve would be enough for the next 100 years. However, given that consumption is expected to increase by 1–2% each year, the current reserve would only cover the next 70 years.[9] The risk posed by the possible exhaustion of resources is substantial. This problem makes countries even more eager to explore new energy options and, for instance, to get access to oil and gas reserves in the Arctic, taking advantages of the effects of climate change and the melting of the icecap. Indeed experts project that the ice could effectively disappear in summer within the next 20–40 years, which would then make the exploitation of Arctic resources technically feasible and therefore more likely.[10] Territorial claims from the Arctic Ocean's bordering countries, i.e. Canada, Denmark, Norway, Russia and the US, highlight how the threat from possible exhaustion of resources makes competition for natural resources fiercer and has an impact on diplomatic relations.

Politicisation of energy

In the case of energy deals, the rules of the market do not always follow traditional patterns, as governments have the tendency to interfere and to use energy and natural resources as a bargaining tool to foster their political agendas. The long-standing gas dispute between Russia and Ukraine saw a new phase of supply disruptions in January 2009 and was arguably fuelled by underlying political motives. The cuts, which followed the inability of Russian Gazprom and Ukrainian Naftohaz Ukrainy to agree on price levels for 2009, affected 12 EU member states and six non-EU countries, including those that rely almost entirely on gas supplies coming from Ukraine, such as Bulgaria and Slovakia. Moscow's objective to retain a strong position of influence is often being pursued through economic tactics, leading some commentators to speculate that the Russian decision to disrupt the gas supply was aimed at punishing NATO (and EU) members for supporting enlargement to include Georgia and Ukraine, and Ukrainian President Kateryna Yushchenko for pursuing pro-Western policies – as well as for supporting Georgia during the Russia–Georgia conflict of August 2008.[11] In spring 2010 President Dmitry Medvedev signed an agreement with Ukraine according to which Russia would reduce the price of natural gas sold to Ukraine by 30% in exchange for a 25-year lease extension of the Russian naval base in Sevastopol.[12] Reminiscent of the Russia–Ukraine dispute was Moscow's decision to cut oil supplies to Belarus in December 2009, sparking fears of disruption across Europe, especially in Poland and Germany as the two countries rely on Belarus for 75% and 10% of their oil needs respectively.[13] All in all, even though it cannot be denied that the threat of supply disruption has now become an annual recurrence, there are two encouraging elements: firstly, unlike gas, oil does not depend on fixed pipelines and it can be shipped using tankers from around the world, hence the risk of oil shortages for European countries is less likely to materialise. Secondly, analysts do not expect another gas dispute between Russia and Ukraine in the near future. This forecast is backed by the introduction by the International Monetary Fund of new loan conditions that would make it easier for Kiev to pay for its supplies.

Transit security

Internal security concerns in a producing or transit country can affect energy supply to the European Union. The Russia–Georgia conflict of August 2008 serves as a case in point. More than a million barrels of oil transit through Georgia every day towards Europe, together with about 26% of Europe's natural gas imports. During the conflict, Russian missiles were fired against the Baku–Tbilisi–Ceyhan (BTC) pipeline, which is one of the main efforts in the attempt to reduce Europe's energy dependence on Russian supplies. At the time of the conflict analysts everywhere had to reassess the risk perception surrounding the BTC pipeline as a transit route for Caspian oil and gas. Indeed, events similar to those of summer 2008 might slow down other projects that would secure non-Russian alternatives for energy supply.[14] Among the most notable of these is the construction of the planned Nabucco natural-gas pipeline from Turkey to Austria, which has been delayed several times, and is now expected to be completed in 2015. At the time of writing, the project was benefiting from a renewed interest and US support. Yet, the issue of finding a definite source of supply remained.[15] Also of concern is the fact that the BTC pipeline passes through the Kurdish region of Turkey, where the threat of separatist violence and sabotage heightens security concerns.

Pipelines are inherently vulnerable. Even though they run mainly underground, their locations are clearly marked, making them easy targets. Attackers can damage facilities by using mechanical means (explosives) or by launching cyber attacks on computer control systems. Pipelines are also vulnerable to indirect attacks. Attacks against telecommunications networks and electricity grids can be disruptive to pipeline networks. Since the early 2000s a number of attacks against oil and gas pipelines have been reported in Colombia, Nigeria, Pakistan, Iraq and Myanmar. In 2002, authorities thwarted an attack planned by al-Qaeda sympathisers in Saudi Arabia. Had it been successful, it would have resulted in the disruption of over 6% of the world's daily oil consumption. Several largely unsuccessful attacks against oil facilities followed, such as the attempted attack on the world's largest oil-processing plant at

Abqaiq in 2006. The risk posed to oil facilities remains tangible, as demonstrated by the arrest in March 2010 of over 100 suspected al-Qaeda militants who were believed to be involved in the planning of attacks against facilities in Saudi Arabia's Eastern Province.[16] In Europe, the most notable example involves a foiled series of bomb attacks planned against gas pipelines by the Irish Republican Army in 1996.[17]

Technical failure

In the summer of 2003 an electricity blackout paralysed Italy and southern Switzerland for nine hours. This was the most significant case of technical failure affecting energy supply in Europe in recent years, affecting as it did about 55m people. A report by Swiss authorities concluded that the main cause of the outage was a fault in the Lukmanier electricity transmission line and the inability to restore it.[18] The same year another blackout struck southeast England, affecting about 500,000 people. Again, the cause was the lack of effective maintenance of the infrastructure. It is clear that regardless of how advanced a country is the risk of technical failure is real. Failure can be caused by extreme weather conditions, such as the January 2009 storm in France, inadequate technical support available for the maintenance of national grids as a result of insufficient capital investment in that work, and from general poor conditions of the systems.

The challenges to EU energy security
External over-reliance and attempts to diversify supplies

EU countries rely very heavily on Russia, the Middle East and North Africa for energy supplies. As demand is also increasing in other regions of the world such as Latin America, South and East Asia, the EU is faced by increasing competition for the acquisition of energy and natural resources. This trend –

Figure 2: **Russia–Europe Gas Pipeline Map**[20]

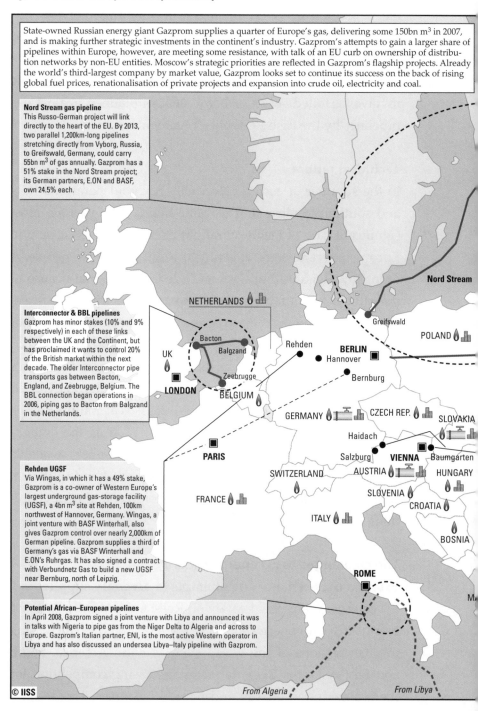

State-owned Russian energy giant Gazprom supplies a quarter of Europe's gas, delivering some 150bn m^3 in 2007, and is making further strategic investments in the continent's industry. Gazprom's attempts to gain a larger share of pipelines within Europe, however, are meeting some resistance, with talk of an EU curb on ownership of distribution networks by non-EU entities. Moscow's strategic priorities are reflected in Gazprom's flagship projects. Already the world's third-largest company by market value, Gazprom looks set to continue its success on the back of rising global fuel prices, renationalisation of private projects and expansion into crude oil, electricity and coal.

Nord Stream gas pipeline
This Russo-German project will link directly to the heart of the EU. By 2013, two parallel 1,200km-long pipelines stretching directly from Vyborg, Russia, to Greifswald, Germany, could carry 55bn m^3 of gas annually. Gazprom has a 51% stake in the Nord Stream project; its German partners, E.ON and BASF, own 24.5% each.

Interconnector & BBL pipelines
Gazprom has minor stakes (10% and 9% respectively) in each of these links between the UK and the Continent, but has proclaimed it wants to control 20% of the British market within the next decade. The older Interconnector pipe transports gas between Bacton, England, and Zeebrugge, Belgium. The BBL connection began operations in 2006, piping gas to Bacton from Balgzand in the Netherlands.

Rehden UGSF
Via Wingas, in which it has a 49% stake, Gazprom is a co-owner of Western Europe's largest underground gas-storage facility (UGSF), a 4bn m^3 site at Rehden, 100km northwest of Hannover, Germany. Wingas, a joint venture with BASF Winterhall, also gives Gazprom control over nearly 2,000km of German pipeline. Gazprom supplies a third of Germany's gas via BASF Winterhall and E.ON's Ruhrgas. It has also signed a contract with Verbundnetz Gas to build a new UGSF near Bernburg, north of Leipzig.

Potential African–European pipelines
In April 2008, Gazprom signed a joint venture with Libya and announced it was in talks with Nigeria to pipe gas from the Niger Delta to Algeria and across to Europe. Gazprom's Italian partner, ENI, is the most active Western operator in Libya and has also discussed an undersea Libya–Italy pipeline with Gazprom.

Nord Stream

NETHERLANDS

Greifswald

POLAND

Bacton
Balgzand
Rehden
BERLIN
UK
Hannover
Zeebrugge
Bernburg
LONDON
BELGIUM
GERMANY
CZECH REP.
SLOVAKIA
Haidach
PARIS
Salzburg
VIENNA
Baumgarten
SWITZERLAND
AUSTRIA
HUNGARY
FRANCE
SLOVENIA
CROATIA
ITALY
BOSNIA
ROME

© IISS

From Algeria
From Libya

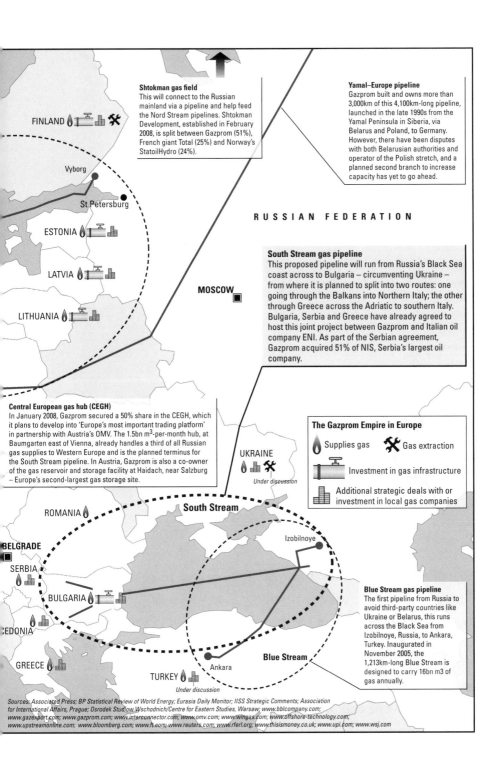

Shtokman gas field
This will connect to the Russian mainland via a pipeline and help feed the Nord Stream pipelines. Shtokman Development, established in February 2008, is split between Gazprom (51%), French giant Total (25%) and Norway's StatoilHydro (24%).

Yamal–Europe pipeline
Gazprom built and owns more than 3,000km of this 4,100km-long pipeline, launched in the late 1990s from the Yamal Peninsula in Siberia, via Belarus and Poland, to Germany. However, there have been disputes with both Belarusian authorities and operator of the Polish stretch, and a planned second branch to increase capacity has yet to go ahead.

FINLAND

Vyborg

St Petersburg

RUSSIAN FEDERATION

ESTONIA

LATVIA

MOSCOW

LITHUANIA

South Stream gas pipeline
This proposed pipeline will run from Russia's Black Sea coast across to Bulgaria – circumventing Ukraine – from where it is planned to split into two routes: one going through the Balkans into Northern Italy; the other through Greece across the Adriatic to southern Italy. Bulgaria, Serbia and Greece have already agreed to host this joint project between Gazprom and Italian oil company ENI. As part of the Serbian agreement, Gazprom acquired 51% of NIS, Serbia's largest oil company.

Central European gas hub (CEGH)
In January 2008, Gazprom secured a 50% share in the CEGH, which it plans to develop into 'Europe's most important trading platform' in partnership with Austria's OMV. The 1.5bn m³-per-month hub, at Baumgarten east of Vienna, already handles a third of all Russian gas supplies to Western Europe and is the planned terminus for the South Stream pipeline. In Austria, Gazprom is also a co-owner of the gas reservoir and storage facility at Haidach, near Salzburg – Europe's second-largest gas storage site.

The Gazprom Empire in Europe

Supplies gas   Gas extraction

Investment in gas infrastructure

Additional strategic deals with or investment in local gas companies

UKRAINE
Under discussion

ROMANIA

South Stream

BELGRADE

SERBIA

Izobilnoye

BULGARIA

CEDONIA

Blue Stream gas pipeline
The first pipeline from Russia to avoid third-party countries like Ukraine or Belarus, this runs across the Black Sea from Izobilnoye, Russia, to Ankara, Turkey. Inaugurated in November 2005, the 1,213km-long Blue Stream is designed to carry 16bn m3 of gas annually.

GREECE

TURKEY   Ankara   Blue Stream
Under discussion

Sources: Associated Press; BP Statistical Review of World Energy; Eurasia Daily Monitor; IISS Strategic Comments; Association for International Affairs, Prague; Osrodek Studiow Wschodnich/Centre for Eastern Studies, Warsaw; www.bblcompany.com; www.gazexport.com; www.gazprom.com; www.interconnector.com; www.omv.com; www.wingas.com; www.offshore-technology.com; www.upstreamonline.com; www.bloomberg.com; www.ft.com; www.reuters.com; www.rferl.org; www.thisismoney.co.uk; www.upi.com; www.wsj.com

Table 1: **EU Crude Oil/Petroleum Product Imports (2007)**

	% of Total Energy Consumption derived from Crude Oil/ Petroleum Products	% Import Dependency Crude Oil/Petroleum products	% of Total Crude Oil/ Petroleum Product Imports supplied by Russia	% of Total Crude Oil/ Petroleum Product Imports supplied by OPEC
Austria	41.1	92.6	1.7	31.6
Belgium	39.4	97.4	31.8	19.7
Bulgaria	24.9	100.8	52.5	1.6
Cyprus	96	98.6	0.9	3.9
Czech Republic	21.7	96.2	44.3	2.5
Denmark	40.6	-67.9	7.1	4.5
Estonia	19.2	99	32.4	0
Finland	29.3	97.8	69.4	0
France	33.6	98.7	15.9	28.5
Germany	33.2	94.3	26	15.3
Greece	51.5	100.9	28.5	50.5
Hungary	28.2	82.7	80.3	0
Ireland	54.9	97	0	1.7
Italy	43.8	92.5	20	55.3
Latvia	34.1	98.1	17.8	0
Lithuania	30.2	93.3	88.4	0
Luxembourg	62.3	98.8	0	0
Malta	100	100	0	0
Netherlands	44	92.8	21.1	20.1
Poland	25.6	102.2	72.1	0.01
Portugal	54	98.9	0.7	44.6
Romania	25.6	53.7	48.3	11
Slovakia	21.3	91.3	82.6	0
Slovenia	35.2	98.9	0.3	0
Spain	48.2	99.7	18.6	35.4
Sweden	27.6	96.7	25	6.3
UK	35.6	0.9	11.4	15.5
EU27	36.4	82.6	24.6	24.2

Source: Calculated from Eurostat Statistics Database: 2007 figures[26]

together with the realisation that it is almost impossible for European countries to achieve energy independence – raises the issue of diversification of energy sources and supply routes.

While EU total import dependency is very high – 82.6% for oil and 60.3% for natural gas – dependency levels vary considerably from country to country (see Figure 2 and Tables 1 and 2 above). On one end of the spectrum there is Denmark, which is an exporting country. At the other are countries which could

Table 2: **EU Natural Gas Imports (2007)**

	% of Total Energy Consumption derived from Natural Gas	% Import Dependency Natural Gas	% Of Total Natural Gas Imports Supplied By Russia	% Of Total Natural Gas Imports Supplied By Algeria	% Of Total Natural Gas Imports Supplied By Nigeria	% Of Total Natural Gas Imports Supplied By Libya
Austria	20.6	81	57	0	0	0
Belgium	26	99.8	4.5	0	0	0
Bulgaria	14.8	91.5	100	0	0	0
Cyprus	0	0	0	0	0	0
Czech Republic	15.5	93.7	77.7	0	0	0
Denmark	19.8	-99.7	0	0	0	0
Estonia	13.3	100	100	0	0	0
Finland	9.9	100	100	0	0	0
France	14.2	96.5	13.5	17.7	7.2	0
Germany	22.6	80.6	43.2	0	0	0
Greece	10	99.6	76.6	23.4	0	0
Hungary	39.6	79.9	74.1	0	0	0
Ireland	27	91.4	0	0	0	0
Italy	37.9	87	30.7	33.2	0	12.5
Latvia	28.5	96.8	100	0	0	0
Lithuania	31.6	102.9	100	0	0	0
Luxembourg	25.8	100	0	0	0	0
Malta	0	0	0	0	0	0
Netherlands	39.5	64.3	0	0	0	0
Poland	12.6	66.7	67.6	0	0	0
Portugal	14.7	98.7	0	34	66	0
Romania	32.4	29.8	91.3	0	0	0
Slovakia	28.2	97.9	99.2	0	0	0
Slovenia	12.4	99.7	51.1	32.2	0	0
Spain	21.7	98.9	0	37.3	23.7	2.2
Sweden	1.8	100	0	0	0	0
UK	37.1	20.3	0	2	0	0
EU27	23.9	60.3	30.7	12.8	3.9	2.5

Source: Calculated from Eurostat Statistics Database: 2007 figures[27]

not survive without external supplies, such as Malta and Greece (both 100% reliant on foreign oil). However, energy vulnerability also has to take into consideration a country's energy mix. In other words, while Sweden is 100% reliant on foreign natural gas because it produces none of its own, gas amounts to just 1.8% of Swedish total energy consumption, meaning that disruption in the supply of foreign gas would have a limited

impact. The same goes for oil: while Sweden relies almost
entirely on foreign imports, oil and petroleum products represent less than a third of total energy consumption. Cyprus, on
the other hand, does not use natural gas but relies on oil for 96%
of its energy consumption, 98.6% of which comes from foreign
suppliers. This places Cyprus in a very vulnerable position. A
different level of vulnerability is represented by countries that
have a rather varied energy mix but rely almost entirely on one
supplier. For instance, Lithuania relies on oil for 30.2% of its
total consumption and on gas for 31.6%; however, it depends
on Russian supplies for 88.4% of its imports of the former and
100% of the latter.[19]

Russia is the leading gas producer and exporter in the
world, and ranks second in oil exports. Here the energy infrastructure is largely in the hands of the government and is
run, when not directly by the government, by entrepreneurs
who have very close ties with the Kremlin. This heightens the
tendency to use energy superiority for political purposes and
to underline Russia's claim to be a major force in international
relations. For these reasons, a number of countries especially in
Central and Eastern Europe are sceptical of Russia's reliability.
The degree of reliance on Russian energy varies considerably
among member states.[21]

Russia, however, is not the only energy supplier for the
EU. Indeed, countries from Central Asia and the Caspian and
Black Sea regions are rich in oil and natural gas and Europeans
are looking at these producers in an attempt to diversify
their supply routes. Initiatives in this direction include the
1995 Interstate Oil and Gas Transport to Europe programme
(Inogate) and the Baku Initiative. However, Gazprom appears
determined to continue its domination over the production
and supply of oil and gas in the region and, given that nearly
all Caspian crude oil travels through Russian infrastructure, it

is not difficult to maintain control. At present, two oil pipeline projects – the Caspian Pipeline Consortium and the BTC – and one gas pipeline project, the South Caucasus Gas Pipeline are at the core of EU's energy diversification as they have the potential to shift the energy flow from the North–South axis to an East–West one. The planned Nabucco and the Trans-Caspian gas pipelines will add to diversification.[22]

Another part of the diversification process concerns energy supplies from the Middle East and North Africa. In 2004, the EU relied on this region for nearly 30% of its oil imports (from Saudi Arabia, Libya and Iran) and about 15% of its gas (primarily from Algeria and, to a lesser degree, from Libya to Italy).[23] Ties with the region are becoming stronger and two new gas pipelines from Algeria to Italy and Spain are being built.[24] Yet, two issues limit the diversification effort in the Middle East and North Africa. The first is the high level of political instability in the region. Second is the attempt by Russia to take part in future Algerian oil and gas projects, which would also include liquefied natural gas (LNG). The LNG market recently saw the entry of the EU's third main outside gas supplier, Norway,[25] which holds significant gas reserves in the Norwegian and Barents Seas together with oil in the North Sea. The LNG developments are clearly a positive sign for the EU's diversification plans and oil production is expected to remain stable in the long term, but other options need to be explored to end over-reliance on Russian supplies.

Limited indigenous production

Data from a recent European Commission report shows that the EU's indigenous production of energy has been in decline since 2004. This further jeopardises the chances for reducing reliance on external suppliers.[28] One way of reducing the Union's external reliance would be by investing more heavily

Table 3: **Upper and lower estimates of EU proved reserves of fossil fuels**

	Crude oil, million barrels of oil	Natural gas, billion m³	Hard coal, billion tonnes	Lignite, million tonnes
Austria	50	20	-	0-20
Bulgaria	15	5	5-100	2,000-2,200
Czech Republic	15	5	1,700-3,200	200-3,500
Denmark	1,200-1,500	70-120	-	-
France	120	10	-	-
Germany	300-370	160-260	100-180	6,600-40,800
Greece	-	-	-	3,900
Hungary	20	10-60	200-280	2,600-3,200
Ireland	-	10-20	15	-
Italy	600-830	90-160	20	-
Lithuania	15	-	-	-
Netherlands	100	1,300-1,400	0-500	-
Norway	7,800-8,500	2,300-3,000	30	-
Poland	100-370	100-170	6,000-14,000	1,500-3,900
Portugal	-	-	-	30
Romania	480-920	60-630	20	410-470
Slovakia	-	15	40	170-260
Slovenia	-	-	-	230
Spain	150	5	200-500	30-330
United Kingdom	3,600-5,500	410-680	160-220	-
World	**1,200,000-1,330,000**	**175,000-182,000**	**479,000-736,000**	**152,000-430,000**

(Source: EC-JRC Institute for Energy, August 2008.)

in indigenous production and increasing the focus on renewable and alternative sources, as well as on so-called 'clean coal' technology. Decisions on how to balance the energy mix are based almost exclusively on the interests of national governments and companies, resulting in great differences among members states. However, growing concerns over the negative environmental impact of energy consumption have sparked new interest at the EU level in favour of reducing carbon and greenhouse-gas emissions via the promotion of environmentally friendly energy sources.

Renewable energy, such as bio-mass, wind, solar and hydro-electricity, provides around 7% of current EU's consumption and is used for heat and electricity generation. Countries such as Germany, Sweden and the UK are championing wind-power generation; while the Czech Republic and Portugal are investing in solar facilities and Austria and Latvia are developing hydro-power facilities. In addition, bio-fuels are gaining greater prominence: the EU is aiming for 10% of all EU transport fuel to come from bio-fuels by 2020. More investments, however, are needed to meet the 2020 targets in terms of reduction of CO_2 emissions and to increase uptake of renewable energy.

While renewable power technology lags behind conventional sources, governments have had to reconsider their decision to phase-out nuclear power as, despite safety concerns, it remains 'the largest single source of low-carbon electricity in the EU'.[29] As of 1 October 2010 there are 195 nuclear plants spread across 17 member states, and indigenous nuclear energy could play a pivotal role in reducing EU's CO_2 emission as well as limiting dependence on external suppliers.[30] In addition, the International Energy Agency (IEA)'s estimates confirm that nuclear energy is cheaper than coal in ten countries and cheaper than gas in all but one member state.[31] This renewed interest in civilian nuclear power may amount to a *nuclear renaissance* and, unsurprisingly, it has raised concerns over the risk of nuclear proliferation and the ability of several countries to access large quantities of plutonium. In particular, Fast Breeder Reactors (FBRs) can function by using very small amounts of uranium, in turn producing vast quantities of plutonium to be used for other reactors or indeed other purposes. This has sparked fears that any country running FBRs could be a potential prolifera-tor and that terrorists could put their hands on the plutonium and use readily available, non-classified knowledge to build and detonate a device.[32] It should be pointed out, however, that FBRs, which are a type of Fast Neutron Reactors, are not a new development. They were first introduced in the early 1950s and currently the US, the UK, France, Japan, India and Russia possess them while China and South Korea are experi-menting with prototypes (Germany also had a short-lived FBR development programme that was shut down in 1991).[33] At present FBRs remain expensive to build and, according to the World Nuclear Association, they could only really be justified if the prices of uranium were to reach pre-1980 values, which are considerably higher than current prices. In spite of these obstacles, Russia is to reconfigure its BN-600 reactors and is improving its BN-800s (with a couple of units being sold to China). Future Russian reactors will include an integrated core aimed at reducing the potential of weapon proliferation from plutonium-239.[34] One of the latest examples of the renewed interest in nuclear energy was the announcement in September 2010 by the German government that it would keep some nuclear power plants in production until the 2030s. This move overruled an earlier decision to phase out the plants by 2021. According to Chancellor Angela Merkel, nuclear energy is to be seen as a 'bridge technology' until renewable energy options become more viable, and for this reason energy companies will now be expected to contribute towards the development of renewables through the payment of a nuclear fuel tax.[35]

In spite of environmental concerns, coal and lignite represent 80% of the EU's fossil-fuel reserves and, regardless of the fact that coal burning accounts for 25% of CO_2 emissions, the abundance of solid fuel makes it likely to remain the fuel of choice for the foreseeable future. Demand is expected to remain constant until 2030, even if domestic production continues its present rate of decline.[36]

Integration into an EU energy market

The debate over the liberalisation of the energy market is ongoing. While many advocate the view that the establishment of a common EU market would increase supply security and would be more cost efficient, there are counter claims that national protectionism insulates countries from the unpredictable swings of the free market. The European Commission first introduced the concept of an EU-wide electricity and gas market in the mid-1990s, but countries such as France, Germany and Spain have always opposed such initiatives. One underlying cause of such opposition is the role played by energy industries in certain member states, where they exert a very strong influence and require their home governments to protect their interests. A potential breakthrough took place in June 2009 when Commission President José Manuel Barroso announced a 'major step towards a truly integrated European energy market'[37] in the form of new rules that would help the Union deal with climate change, increased dependence on foreign suppliers and global competitiveness. Among other changes, the new regulations aim at increasing cross-border cooperation, market transparency, protection of vulnerable consumers and energy efficiency. Member states have been given 18 months to transpose the directives into national law. Although this clearly represents a positive development, progress could be influenced by the debate over whether the internal market would be able to guarantee efficient supply and infrastructure security. These changes are still at consultation stage and are expected to be endorsed by 2011.

Medium- and long-term trends

A number of medium- and long-term trends can be identified with regards to patterns of diversification of energy supply and reduction of carbon emissions. The EU's dependence on imported fossil fuels will more likely increase than diminish. Indeed, the percentage of EU gas consumption derived from imports is expected to increase to more than 80% by 2030, while the dependency on imported crude oil and petroleum products is predicted to increase to 93% over the same period.[38] The environmental costs might become greater than ever in the absence of effective mitigating strategies. Even if CO_2 emissions are stabilised at 1990 levels in compliance with the Kyoto Protocol, greenhouse gasses will continue rise until the end of the century, worsening global warming. The rates of deforestation will also affect this trend.[39]

Diversification is likely to prove very challenging. Some experts estimate that by 2020 the EU will rely on Russia for more than 40% of its natural gas.[40] It is questionable whether member states will manage to agree on a common approach towards Russia and to push Gazprom to agree to the principles of competition in place in Europe. In particular, they would need to convince Moscow to ratify the Energy Charter Treaty and to accept foreign investments in its energy sector.[41] In addition, bilateral agreements such as those between Russia and Germany are most likely to increase the EU's dependence on Russian supplies.

The Caspian region is expected to continue to be a major supplier of energy, especially of natural gas, to Europe. However, it is questionable whether the Caspian countries will continue to see the EU as a prime customer for oil exports. Given that demand in Europe is expected to grow by little more than 1m barrels a day (b/d) in the next ten to 15 years – compared to the growth of 10m b/d expected in the Asian market over the same period – it is to be expected that producers in the Caspian region will prefer to sell their oil eastward in more lucrative markets.[42] Yet, some critics maintain that Caspian producers will continue to find sales to the West more appealing given their geographic proximity to Europe.[43]

Diversification towards renewable energy is limited by the abundance of coal (40bn tonnes), which analysts believe will retain a significant role in the EU energy scene in the long run, despite a predicted focus among European governments on energy efficiency, reducing consumption and generating renewable energy.[44] While several member states have begun to revise their stand on nuclear power, it is unlikely that Europe will witness a resurgence of nuclear energy beyond those countries that already have nuclear facilities in place. The costs associated with the construction of new facilities and the issue of nuclear-waste disposal will remain at the core of anti-nuclear arguments. On the other hand, the upgrade and expansion of current facilities is a possibility. Notably, Russia has recently proposed a joint nuclear generation project with Ukraine and showed willingness to play a role in upgrading Ukrainian reactors.[45]

Conclusions

European energy security is threatened by a number of risks and threats. The approach to those risks varies according to countries' understating of the concept of 'energy security'. The challenges that need to be overcome are substantial and no quick fix is available. Above all, there is a clear need for a united approach; Europe should speak with a single voice when it comes to energy.

Russia will continue to be the EU's main energy supplier for years to come, therefore the establishment of healthy economic relations is in the interest of both Europeans and of Russia itself. In addition, it is only through cooperation that member states can hope to be able to deal with Russia on an equal footing and to exercise any kind of leverage on Gazprom. Given the EU's inability to wean itself from a dependence on energy imports, Europeans will have to rely on external sources, often in volatile countries, which will create a tension between the fundamental principles of the EU's security strategy – the nexus between human security, security and development – and the need to secure good energy deals in the face of growing demand from other customers. The EU needs a common energy strategy and a common policy on subsidies for renewable sources. Europeans should focus on fostering relations with new and potential energy suppliers and transit countries, with the goal of establishing a balanced commercial relationship. At present, energy policy is still driven by national-level approaches, which stand in the way of a common energy strategy. If this can be curbed, it would result in better economic deals for the Union as a whole with decreased political vulnerability. More could be done to reduce emissions and protect the environment. In part, this depends of the level of subsidy member states are willing to offer for new technologies used in the production of renewable resources. Aside from the environmental effects, new energy sources reduce dependence on external producers. In general, the EU must bring together economic and political experts so that future policy can incorporate the security aspects of energy issues.

Concluding Remarks

Bastian Giegerich

On 7 September 2010, President of the European Commission José Manuel Barroso gave his first-ever 'state of the union' address to the European Parliament. During his speech he made the case for a more united approach to foreign and security policy:

> I am impatient to see the Union play the role in global affairs that matches its economic weight ... If we don't act together, Europe will not be a force in the world ... To be effective on the international stage, we need the weight of the European Union. Size matters, now more than ever.[1]

The contributions to this volume echo that sentiment – at least in the sense that the complexities of the contemporary security environment are already overwhelming the abilities of the nation-state to provide security on its own. A comprehensive security approach, global in its outlook, driven by closer cooperation of EU member-state governments and EU-level institutions, must be the goal, even though it is clear that many important areas of security policy will continue to remain the prerogative of national governments. However, EU capacity for action still falls short of the demands generated by current and future security challenges. Several chapters point out that the national level is increasingly unable to provide adequate policy solutions and yet continues to dominate. European rhetoric is running ahead of the ability to act on the global stage. Such a state of affairs might become dangerous if third parties do not recognise the difference between oratory and capacity to deliver.[2]

François Heisbourg suggests that the gap between EU capabilities and EU aspirations is highly visible in Europe's relations with great powers. The fact that the EU does not have competencies in the security and defence area is a major obstacle in the attempt to actively shape great-power relations. The normative attractiveness of the Union does not translate into leverage in those dealings and condemns the EU to a reactive policy pattern. Heisbourg argues that, for the time being, the EU is at best an issue-specific great power, in those areas where EU member-states can generate and maintain a common position.

The same kind of underperformance was also observed in the area of civilian and military crisis-management capabilities where member-state governments do not implement agreed goals. While one can certainly observe much operational activity, both in the civilian and military realms, deployments do not seem to follow an overall strategy. Prioritising and mobilising what limited resources are available for EU conflict prevention and crisis-management missions, especially after the financial and economic crisis of 2008–09, will remain difficult in the absence of such strategic guidance.[3]

The EU's policy in the area of WMD proliferation is a case where its normative dimension as a 'good non-proliferation citizen', as Ben Rhode argues, could be an important plank strengthening international non-proliferation regimes through the power of example. However, the practical engagement with Iran on its nuclear programme demonstrates that in trying to fill an international vacuum, the EU failed to make headway after initial progress. In fact, Rhode warns, Iran raises the possibility of large-scale policy failure which would put the EU's WMD proliferation strategy under severe pressure and undermine the normative stance that is underpinning this strategy.

The analysis of demographic trends and their security implications by Christopher Langton revealed that policy responses in the EU do not do justice to the complexity of the issue. Faced with a genuinely transnational issue, EU member states remain locked into national answers. Against the backdrop of ageing and shrinking populations in many EU member states, welfare issues dominate the agenda while the wider security implications, likely to be exacerbated by climate change, remain ill understood. The problem of distinctly national responses to a transnational problem is also addressed by Virginia Comolli in her chapter on energy security. Energy security's many facets prevent a common interpretation and energy dependency takes on many different forms for individual member states. Robert Whalley's work on critical infrastructure also points to increased complexity in the sense that what counts as critical infrastructure, where it is located, and who owns it has changed dramatically from a time when governments had firm control of such assets. Increasing links between societies would seem to amount to increasing vulnerabilities. Yet that planning assumption of greater risks in the future, so far, has not translated into a more networked approach. Thus, on demographics and migration, energy security and critical infrastructure, the complexity of truly transnational threats is not yet acknowledged. Common European responses would be better able to respond to the nature of the threats.

The promise of greater cooperation does not, however, apply in equal measure to all areas under consideration. In dealing with terrorism, European security services have focused on transnational Islamist terrorism while at the same time trying to contain more traditional threats to Europe. As Nigel Inkster argues, European member states do not command a common counter-terrorism tool kit and have vastly different capabilities. As a whole, Europe remains dangerously dependent on the US for intelligence – a situation which may turn into a political liability. On the other hand, the nature of the security services' work imposes limits on what can be done at the EU level. As a result, Inkster argues, the most that would be possible is to see the EU as an enabling policy arena for effective national responses.

Yet another set of problems presents itself in the area of extreme environmental events analysed by Jeffrey Mazo. As he points out, such events are wild cards – often unexpected, usually with a low probability of occurring within a given time-frame but of serious consequence if they do. However, they have to be seen in relation to the systemic stress caused by climate change, which is likely to increase both the frequency and the severity of extreme environmental events. Threat perceptions regarding environmental risks seem to be driven by either chronic or immediate problems, which means these synergetic effects are likely to be missed. While extreme environmental events are difficult to plan for by their very nature, enhanced communication and coordination across the EU is likely make responses more effective.

Lisbon to the rescue?

Many observers attached high hopes to the Lisbon Treaty because several of its stipulations explicitly aimed at making the EU a more effective and coherent actor in the security field. Lisbon formulated several political aspirations for the EU as a security actor, which find their expression in institutional change. However, once more, moving from aspiration to implementation requires political investment; as implementation of the Lisbon provisions was getting under way in 2010 it increasingly looked as if member states still lacked the political will to make use of the new instruments and guidance provided by the treaty.

The first innovations of note relate to two senior positions created by the Lisbon Treaty. The role of president of the European Council was to rid the EU of the inconsistencies and inefficiencies created by the previous model of the six-monthly rotating presidency with a two-and-a-half-year mandate, renewable once. The president is tasked with generating consensus in the Council, the body through which EU member governments make decisions, and represent the Union on matters of foreign and security policy. Former Belgian Prime Minister Herman van Rompuy, who had gained a reputation as an effective deal maker, was appointed to the post in November 2009. The second senior position merged the post of high representative for the EU's Common Foreign and Security Policy (CFSP) and that of the external-relations commissioner. While this merged position straddles the divide between the two key power centres of Commission and Council and its incumbent must, as high representative and simultaneously vice-president of the Commission (HR/VP), report to two masters, the hope is that it will bring greater coherence to the EU's international policies ranging from aid to crisis management. Baroness Catherine Ashton, a former EU trade commissioner, was appointed to the post with a five-year term. Similar to van Rompuy, Ashton brings a reputation as an effective administrator but very little security policy experience to the job.

Both appointments followed intense periods of horse trading where several heavyweight candidates for both posts fell foul of the many criteria that ultimately decide these matters in the EU. Given that the job descriptions are relatively vague, it is likely that personalities will matter greatly. With the two present incumbents, EU member governments chose managers rather than leaders. Neither the current president nor the current HR/VP are expected to represent a serious challenge to member-state dominance in the security policy area, which might ultimately limit their impact in terms of facilitating a greater level of coherence.

Ironically, in the area of security and defence policy the Lisbon treaty has revealed deep divisions among EU member states. It is questionable whether the treaty innovations can unfold a positive effect under these circumstances. Clearly, member-state governments are still overwhelmingly concerned with national sovereignty and for good reasons. No government will find it acceptable to delegate responsibility for national security.

Over the course of the last decade, the EU has developed the decision-making structures and instruments to become a security policy actor beyond its own borders. The EU as a framework for security and defence cooperation has reached a stage where further progress demands closer and innovative forms of collaboration. Without them, the dynamic of the past years is likely to fade away. While there is undeniable process and it is probably fair to say that the security and defence sector represented the policy area that developed most rapidly in the EU during the previous decade, there remains a marked disconnect between the EU's capacity to declare grand ambitions and the union's capacity for delivering on them.

Timeline

1991

9–10 December: Treaty on European Union (TEU) approved at Maastricht (Maastricht Treaty). It establishes the Common Foreign and Security Policy (CFSP) and changes the name of the EEC to the European Community, which forms one of the three pillars of the EU.

1992

19 June: WEU Petersberg Summit: Adoption of the Petersberg Declaration (which includes the Petersberg Tasks).

1993

1 November: The Maastricht Treaty enters into force.

1997

16–17 June: European Council agrees on Treaty of Amsterdam, which revises the Maastricht Treaty. The revision incorporates the Petersberg Tasks into the EU and creates the post of the Secretary-General of the Council/High Representative for the CFSP.

1998

3–4 December: France and the UK issue the St Malo Declaration, which paves the way for new initiatives on security and defence policy within the EU.

1999

24 March – 10 June: Kosovo War: NATO Operation Allied Force

1 May: Amsterdam Treaty enters into force.

3–4 June: At the European Council meeting in Cologne, EU member states decide to develop structures and procedures for a European Security and Defence Policy (ESDP) within the context of CFSP and develop capabilities to undertake crisis-management operations.

10–11 December: At its meeting in Helsinki, the European Council defines the goal of being able to deploy within 60 days and to sustain for one year 50–60,000 military personnel for crisis-management operations. This goal, to be reached by 2003, became known as the Helsinki Headline Goal.

2000

7–11 December: At the European Council meeting in Nice, permanent bodies to run ESDP are set up: the Political and Security Committee, the EU Military Committee and the EU Military Staff. Member states also adopt the Treaty of Nice, another revision of the Treaty on European Union.

2001

11 September: Terrorist attacks against New York and Washington, DC.

7 October: Military operations against the Taliban Government in Afghanistan begin.

2002

16 December: NATO and the EU sign a formal cooperation agreement.

2003

1 January: The first ESDP mission, the EU Police Mission in Bosnia and Herzegovina, is launched.

1 February: The Treaty of Nice enters into force.

20 March: Beginning of Iraq War.

31 March: EU launches its first military operation in Macedonia with NATO support.

5 June: EU launches its first operation outside of the Balkans by agreeing to send a military mission to the Democratic Republic of the Congo at the request of the United Nations.

12–13 December: EU leaders adopt a European Security Strategy (ESS) and the EU Strategy Against Proliferation of Weapons of Mass Destruction.

2004

11 March: Terrorist attacks on commuter trains in Madrid kill 191 people.

25–26 March: EU leaders adopt the Declaration on Combating Terrorism.

17–18 June: EU leaders endorse a new military headline goal with a 2010 timeline (Headline Goal 2010) at their European Council meeting.

29 October: EU heads of state and government sign the Treaty Establishing a Constitution for Europe.

2005

7 July: Suicide bomb attacks on three London underground trains and a bus kill 52 and injure more than 700.

December: EU Counter-Terrorism Strategy Adopted.

2007

13 December: EU leaders sign the Treaty of Lisbon, which aims to reform and modernise EU decision-making structures and processes.

2008

11–12 December: EU report on the implementation of the ESS.

2009

1 December: Treaty of Lisbon enters into force.

GLOSSARY

AQ	al-Qaeda
AQAP	al-Qaeda in the Arabian peninsula
AQIM	al-Qaeda in the Islamic Maghreb
AQM	al-Qaeda in Mesopotamia
BTC	Baku–Tblisi–Ceyhan pipeline
BTWC	Biological and Toxin Weapons Convention
CBRN	chemical, biological, radiological and nuclear weapons
CFSP	Common Foreign and Security Policy
CIRA	Continuity Irish Republican Army
CSDP	Common Security and Defence Policy
CTBT	Comprehensive Test-Ban Treaty
CTBTO	Comprehensive Test-Ban Treaty Organisation
CWC	Chemical Weapons Convention
E3	France, Germany and the UK
E3+3	E3 plus China, Russia and the United States
ELA	Epanastatikos Laikos Agonas
ESS	European Security Strategy
ESDP	European Security and Defence Policy
ETA	Euskadi ta Askatasuna
EU	European Union
FATA	Federally Administered Tribal Areas (Pakistan)

FMCT	Fissile Material Cut-Off Treaty
GIA	Armed Islamic Group of Algeria
GSPC	Salafist Group for Preaching and Combat
IAEA	International Atomic Energy Agency
IEA	International Energy Agency
IfS	Instrument for Stability (EU funding mechanism)
INSC	Instrument for Nuclear Safety Cooperation
IPCC	Intergovernmental Panel on Climate Change
IRA	Irish Republican Army
IRGC	Iranian Revolutionary Guard Corps
JRC	Joint Research Centre (European Commission)
LEU	Low-enriched uranium
LNG	Liquefied natural gas
Mercosur	Common Market of the South (South American trading bloc)
N17	November 17
NATO	North Atlantic Treaty Organisation
NPT	Nuclear Non-proliferation Treaty
OECD	Organisation for Economic Cooperation and Development
OSCE	Organisation for Security and Cooperation in Europe
OPCW	Organisation for the Prohibition of Chemical Weapons
PIRA	Provisional Irish Republican Army
PSCD	Permanent Structured Cooperation on Defence
RIRA	Real Irish Republican Army
WMD	Weapons of mass destruction
UN	United Nations
UNIFIL	United Nations Interim Force in Lebanon
UNSCR	United Nations Security Council Resolution
UVF	Ulster Volunteer Force

NOTES

Introduction

1. Benita Ferrero-Waldner, 'The European Union and the World: A Hard Look at Soft Power', speech at Columbia University, New York, 24 September 2007. Transcript available at http://www.europa-eu-un.org/articles/en/article_7330_en.htm.
2. Martin Ortega, *Building the Future: The EU's Contribution to Global Governance*, Chaillot Paper No. 100 (Paris: EUISS, 2007), p. 93 (emphasis in original).
3. Robert Kagan, *Paradise and Power: America and Europe in the New World Order* (London: Atlantic Books, 2003).
4. European Council, 'A Secure Europe in a Better World: European Security Strategy', 12 December 2003, Brussels, http://www.consilium.europa.eu/uedocs/cmsUpload/78367.pdf; 'European Council Report on the Implementation of the European Security Strategy: Providing Security in a Changing World', 11 December 2008, Brussels, http://www.consilium.europa.eu/ueDocs/cms_Data/docs/pressdata/EN/reports/104630.pdf.
5. Présidence de la République, *Défense et Sécurité Nationale*, Le Livre Blanc, juin 2008, p. 63.
6. Cabinet Office, Security for the Next Generation, *The National Security Strategy of the United Kingdom: Update 2009*, June 2009, p. 5.
7. Cabinet Office, 'A Strong Britain in an Age of Uncertainty', *The National Security Strategy 2009*, October 2009, p. 18.
8. European Council, 'Europe's Attractiveness in a Changing World', Keynote speech by Herman van Rompuy, 2 June 2010, http://www.consilium.europa.eu/uedocs/cms_data/docs/pressdata/en/ec/114883.pdf.
9. *Ibid*.
10. Ferrero Waldner 2007.
11. See UN database: World Population Prospects: The 2008 Revision, http://esa.un.org/UNPP/.
12. See Worldbank database: 'World Development Indicators', http://data.worldbank.org/indicator; D. Wilson and R. Purushothaman, 'Dreaming with BRICs: The Path to 2050', Goldman Sachs Global Economics Paper No. 99, 2003, available at http://www2.goldmansachs.com/ideas/brics/book/99-dreaming.pdf.
13. I. Krastev, 'Russia and the European order: Sovereign democracy explained',

in *American Interest,* vol 4, no. 2, 2008, p. 24.

[14] L.M. Phillips, *International Relations in 2030: The transformative power of large developing countries,* Discussion Paper 2/2008 (Bonn: German Development Institute, 2008), www.die-gdi.de.

[15] G. Grevi, *The interpolar world: a new scenario,* Occasional Paper No. 79, (Paris: EUISS, 2009), p. 9.

[16] N. Gnesotto and G. Grevi, *The New Global Puzzle: What World for the EU in 2025?,* (Paris: EUISS, 2006); C. Grant and T. Valasek, *Preparing for the multi-polar world: European Foreign and Security Policy in 2020* (London: CER, 2007).

[17] See: I. Krastev and M. Leonard, 'The World's Choice: Super, Soft, or Herbivorous Power?', 2007, http://www.opendemocracy.net/article/ibsa_countries.

[18] R. Gowan and F. Brantner, 'A Global Force for Human Rights? An Audit of European Power at the UN', (London: European Council on Foreign Relations, 2008), http://ecfr.3cdn.net/30b67f149cd7aaa888_3xm6bq7ff.pdf.

[19] Emil J. Kirchner, 'European Union: Moving Towards a European Security Culture?', in: E.J. Kirchner and J. Sperling, eds, *National Security Cultures: Patterns of Global Governance* (Abingdon: Routledge, 2010), pp. 103–123.

Chapter One

[1] See Jean-Marie Guehenno, 'Le modèle européen', RAMSES du XXème anniversaire de l'IFRI, Paris, Autumn 1999.

[2] Zaki Laïdi, 'The Normative Empire – The Unintended Consequences of European Power', GARNET Policy Brief, no. 6, February 2008.

[3] See Zaki Laïdi, 'Europe as a Risk Averse Power – a Hypothesis', GARNET Policy Brief no. 1, February 2010.

[4] Déclaration sur le Moyen-Orient faite à Venise le 13 juin 1980. Full text available at www.medea.be/index.html?page=0&lang=fr&doc=52.

[5] Jan Zielonka, *Europe as Empire: the Nature of an Enlarged European Union* (Oxford: Oxford University Press, 2006).

[6] Report of EU High Representative, 'A Secure Europe in a better World – European Security Strategy', European Council, Brussels, 12 December 2003; available at http://www.consilium.europa.eu/showPage.aspx?id=266&lang=en.

[7] Charles Krauthammer, 'The Unipolar moment', *Foreign Affairs,* vol. 70, no. 1, January 1990;

[8] See Madeleine Albright, 'The right balance will secure NATO's Future', *The Financial Times,* 7 December 1998; the US's attitude had shifted by the time President George W. Bush proclaimed 'Let Europe's defence pole advance' in a speech at NATO's Summit in Bucharest on 4 April 2008.

[9] Krastev, 'A Retired Power', *The American Interest,* July–August 2010.

[10] François Godement and John Fox, 'A Power Audit of EU-China Relations', European Council on Foreign Relations, Brussels, 2009.

[11] Lanxin Xiang, 'Chinese outlook on European security: towards ideological

convergence?', in Thierry Tardy, ed., *European Security in a Global Context* (London: Routledge, 2009).

12 See Transcript at www.washington post.com/wp-dyn/content/article/ 2007/02/12/AR2007021200555.html.

13 See Yegor Gaidar, 'Collapse of an Empire: Lessons for Modern Russia' (Washington DC, Brookings Institution, 2008).

14 See 'Russia in the 21ˢᵗ century', INSOR, February 2010 (www.insor-russia.ru/ en), and Sergei Kavaganov, 'Russia's Choice', *Survival*, vol. 52, no. 1, February–March 2010.

15 Ahmet Davutoglu, 'Principles of Turkish Foreign Policy', speech in Washington DC, 8 December 2009 (www.setadc.org)

16 Japanese ODA in 2009: $9.5bn (OECD-DAC figures)

17 See OECD policy brief, October 2007 (www.oecd.org/dataoecd/17/52/ 39452196.pdf). According to the IMF World Economic Outlook database, India's estimated GDP (in PPP) in 2009 was $3526bn, comparable to that of China in 2000. India's foreign trade, at some $387bn, was less than a fifth of China's in 2009, and was greater than that of Switzerland.

18 See Shirish Shranke and Richard Dobbs, 'India vs China', *Financial Times*, 18 May 2010.

19 For details on countries' purchasing power, see the IMF's World Economic

Outlook 2010, 'Recovery Risk and Rebalancing' (Washington DC: IMF, 2010), at http://www.imf.org/external/ pubs/ft/weo/2010/02/index.htm.

20 These are probably underestimates, since they include only registered overseas workers. See Ministry of Overseas Indian Affairs, 'Estimated number of overseas Indians', at www. moia.gov.in/writereaddata/pdf/ NRISPIOS-Data.pdf, which counts 2.7m Indians working in Kuwait, Oman, Qatar and the UAE, out of a combined population of 13.2m. In the UEA (population: 4.7m) there are 1.7m Indian workers. Close to 1.8m Indians live in Saudi Arabia (population 27m). Population estimates from CIA *World Factbook 2010*.

21 Waheguru Pal Singh Sidhu and Christophe Jaffrelot, 'Does Europe matter to India?', in Tardy, ed., *European Security in a Global Context*.

22 As fictionalised in Jean-Christophe Rufin, *Rouge Bresil*, (Paris: Gallimard, 2001).

23 Nicolas von Ondaya and Roderick Parks, 'The EU in the face of disaster', SWP Commentary 9, Berlin, April 2010.

24 Preamble of the Treaty Establishing the European Community, Rome, 25 March 1957. The phrase was coined by Blair's predecessor John Major in his 'Heart of Europe' speech of 7 September 1992.

Chapter Two

1   The EU Security Strategy argued the EU 'could add particular value by developing operations involving both civilian and military capabilities'. European Union, 'A Secure Europe in a Better World: European Security Strategy', 12 December 2003, p. 11.

2   European Union, 'Development of European Military Capabilities', 2010, http://www.consilium.europa.eu/uedocs/cmsUpload/100511UpdatedFactsheet_cap_militaires-v5_EN.pdf.

3   The EU uses a set of scenarios describing the kind of operations it aims to be able to conduct. Each scenario involves a different set of assumptions about strategic planning variables such as the distance of the theatre of operations from Brussels; the time required to reach full operating capability; the duration of the mission; and, for long-term operations, force-rotation arrangements.

4   Javier Solana, 'ESDP@10: What Lessons for the Future?', Document No. S195/09, 28 July 2010, Brussels, http://www.consilium.europa.eu/uedocs/cms_data/docs/pressdata/en/discours/109453.pdf.

5   Nick Witney, 'Re-energising Europe's Security and Defence Policy' (London: European Council on Foreign Relations), 2008.

6   In 2001, several structures have been set up to run important aspects of CSDP and prepare the work of the Council of the EU, the body through which EU member-state governments maintain oversight and provide direction. Key institutions include the Political and Security Committee (PSC) which meets at ambassadorial level, the EU Military Committee, which is composed of the EU member states' chiefs of defence, the EU Military Staff, which provides in-house military expertise to the Council, the Committee for Civilian Aspects of Crisis Management, and the Civilian Planning and Conduct Capability which plans and conducts civilian CSDP operations under the control and direction of the PSC. Further information on these institutions as well as key documents can be found at: http://www.consilium.europa.eu/showPage.aspx?id=261&lang=en.

7   The Petersberg Tasks identified targets in terms of the EU's ability to carry out peacekeeping, rescue, humanitarian and crisis-management missions. They were formally set out in the Petersberg Declaration adopted at the Ministerial Council of the Western European Union in 1992. For more details, see http://europa.eu/scadplus/glossary/petersberg_tasks_en.htm.

8   European Union Helsinki Headline Goal 1999, www.consilium.europa.eu. The Petersberg Tasks included humanitarian and rescue tasks, peacekeeping tasks, and tasks of combat forces in crisis management, including peacemaking. The Treaty of Amsterdam incorporated these tasks within the EU. The European Security Strategy from 2003 and the Treaty of Lisbon entering into force in December 2009 expanded the original task list. The Lisbon Treaty clarifies that the tasks also include disarmament operations, the provision of military advice and assistance to third countries, conflict prevention and post-conflict stabilisation. The treaty furthermore underlines that

all the tasks could be applied in the fight against terrorism and in support of third-country efforts to combat terrorism in their territories.

9   European Union, 'Headline Goal 2010', approved by the General Affairs and External Relations Council on 17 May 2004, endorsed by the European Council of 17–18 June 2004, www.consilium.europa.eu/uedocs/cmsUpload/2010%20Headline%20Goal.pdf.

10 European Union Military Capabilities Commitment Conference, 22 November 2004, www.consilium.europa.eu/uedocs/cmsUpload/MILITARY%20CAPABILITY%20COMMITMENT%20CONFERENCE%2022.11.04.pdf.

11 European Union Military Capabilities Commitment Conference, 22 November 2004, www.consilium.europa.eu/uedocs/cmsUpload/MILITARY%20CAPABILITY%20COMMITMENT%20CONFERENCE%2022.11.04.pdf.

12 Council of the European Union, Capabilities Improvement Chart I/2006, http://www.consilium.europa.eu/uedocs/cms_data/docs/pressdata/en/esdp/89603.pdf.

13 European Union Declaration on Strengthening Capabilities, 11

December 2008, www.consilium.europa.eu/ueDocs/cms_Data/docs/pressData/en/esdp/104676.pdf.

14 In 2009 it was estimated that there were about 1.6m civilian personnel in the EU member states. At the time only about 2,000 were actually deployed. See ISIS, 'Tapping the Human Dimension: Civilian Capabilities in ESDP', European Security Review No. 43, 2009.

15 Daniel Korski and Richard Gowan, 'Can the EU Rebuild Failing States? A review of Europe's Civilian Capabilities' (London: European Council on Foreign Relations, 2009), p. 8.

16 Muriel Asseburg and Ronja Kempin, 'Schlussfolgerungen und Empfehlungen', in Asseburg and Kempin, eds, *Die EU als strategischer Akteur in der Sicherheits- und Verteidigungspolitik? Eine systematische Bestandsaufnahme von ESVP-Missionen und Operationen* (Berlin: SWP, 2009), pp. 164–177.

17 Damien Helly, 'Lessons from EUFOR Tchad/RCA' (Paris: EUISS, 2010).

18 Korski and Gowan (2009), p. 22; A similar conclusion is presented by Asseburg and Kempin (2009), p. 165.

Chapter Three

1   Population Division of the Department of Economic and Social Affairs of the United Nations Secretariat, *World population Prospects: The 2008 Revision*, http://esa.un.org/unpp/.

2   Kate Connolly, 'Angela Merkel Declares Death of German Multiculturalism', *The Guardian*, 17 October 2010.

3   Cabinet Office, *National Security Strategy 2009*, p. 24 http://interactive.cabinetoffice.gov.uk/documents/security/national_security_strategy.pdf.

4   See http://www.migrationdrc.org/publications/briefing_papers/BP12.pdf.

5   G. Lanzieri, 'Population in Europe 2007: first results', eurostat statistics in focus 81/2008.

6   Ibid.

7   Population Division of the Department of Economic and Social Affairs of the United Nations Secretariat, World population Prospects: The 2008 Revision, available at http://esa.un.org/UNPP/.

8   Lanzieri, 'Population in Europe 2007: first results'.

9   OECD, International Migration Outlook 2009, available at http://www.oecd.org/document/4/0,3343,en_2649_33931_43009971_1_1_1_37415,00.html.

10 See http://www.migrationdrc.org/publications/briefing_papers/BP12.pdf.

11 K. Khoser, 'Irregular migration, state security and human security', Global Commission on International Migration, September 2005, www.gcim.org/attachements/TP5.pdf.

12 S. Islam, 'Europe: Crises of Identity', Working Paper Series, International Peace Academy, February 2007, p. 8, at http://www.ipacademy.org/publication/policy-papers/detail/121-europe-crises-of-identity.html.

13 European Union Agency for Fundamental Rights (FRA), Annual Report 2009, 24 June 2009.

14 High Representative and European Commission: Climate Change and International Security, S113/08, 14 March 2008, p. 2.

15 Cabinet Office, 'Security for the Next Generation', The National Security Strategy of the United Kingdom: Update 2009, June 2009.

16 R.K. Pachauri, L.F. Qureshy and K.S. Nesamani, 'Seeking refuge from the environment: the paradox of environmental refugees' in K. Srinivasan and M. Vlassoff, eds, Population-Development Nexus in India: Challenges for the New Millennium, (New Delhi: Tata-McGraw-Hill, 2001), pp. 364–375.

17 Franco Frattini, European Minister responsible for Justice, Freedom and Security, 'Enhanced mobility, vigorous integration strategy, and zero tolerance on illegal employment: a dynamic approach to European immigration policies', speech at High-level Conference on Legal Immigration, Lisbon 13 September 2007, SPEECH/07/526, p. 2. The speech preceded the introduction of the 'Blue Card' scheme in October 2007. The remaining 10% are not classified.

18 T.E. Khromova, M.B. Dyurgerov, and R.G. Barry, 'Late-twentieth century changes in glacier extent in the Ak-shirak Range, Central Asia, determined from historical data and ASTER imagery', Geophysical Research Letters, vol. 30 no. 16, 2003, pp. 1863–68.

19 S. Harrison, 'Kazakhstan: glaciers and geopolitics', 6 September 2007 http://www.opendemocracy.net/globalization-climate_change_debate/kazakhstan_2551.jsp.

20 UN Department of Economic and Social Affairs, 'World Urbanization Prospects: The 2007 Revision', Population Database, http://esa.un.org/unup/.

21 Ibid.

22 'Burden of infectious diseases on migrant health in Europe', European Journal of Public Health, Vol. 15, Supplement 1, 2005, p. 21. Finding from workshop at the 13th EUPHA Conference, 'Promoting the public's health: reorienting health policies, linking health promotion and health care', Graz, 10–12 November 2005.

23 Ömer Taspinar, 'Europe's Muslim Street', March–April 2003, available at http://www.brookings.edu/opinions/ 2003/03middleeast_taspinar.aspx.

Chapter Four

1 B.M. Jenkins, 'International Terrorism: A New Mode of Conflict' in David Carlton and Carlo Schaerf, eds, *International Terrorism and World Security* (London: Croom Helm, 1975), p. 15.

2 Islamist thinkers who have influenced jihadi ideology, such as Sayyid Qutb, author of *Milestones*, explicity reject Westernisation though not modernity per se. Scholarly opinion differs as to whether jihadist terrorism is a backlash against or a product of globalisation and modernity or a consequence of it. In his book *The Search for a New Ummah* (New York: Columbia University Press, 2006) Professor Olivier Roy argues that Islamist ideologues have been prepared to jettison traditional Islamic cultures in seeking to create 'a universal religious identity that transcends the very notion of culture'. More recently Ibrahim al Rubeish, an al-Qaeda in the Arabian Peninsula ideologue, in an audio address on 18 September 2010, warned all Muslims 'concerned about the Ummah in the Land of the Two Holy Places (i.e., Saudi Arabia)' that increasing Westernisation risked obliterating Islamic culture and traditional Muslim values.

3 On November 17 2000 Moinul Abedin, a Bangladeshi national, was arrested in Birmingham in possession of bomb-making instructions, detonators and 100kg of the chemicals required to make the explosive HTMD. Abedin, who was subsequently sentenced to 20 years' imprisonment, gave no indication as to his motivation or intended targets but he was also found in possession of Islamist propaganda materials.

4 Brian Leapman, '4,000 in UK Trained at Terror Camps', *Daily Telegraph* 15 July 2007, citing unnamed British security officials.

5 Nicola Smith and Bojan Pancevski, 'German Militants Seen in Taliban Border Unit', *Sunday Times*, 1 October 2010, citing unnamed German officials.

6 Thomas Jocelyn, 'The Long War Journal', 30 September 2009.

7 See http:www.longwarjournal.org/ pakistan-strikes.php.

8 Henry McDonald, 'Survey Shows Some Support for Real IRA', *The Guardian*, 6 October 2010.

9 'Man Jailed Over Nail Bombs Plot', BBC News, 25 June 2008.

10 David Leppard, 'Bomb Seizures Spark Far-right Terror Plot Fear', *Sunday Times*, 5 July 2009.

11 James Brandon, 'Unlocking al Qaeda: Islamist Extremism in British Prisons', The Quilliam Foundation, November 2009.

12 For details of the Contest Strategy see HM Government, *The United Kingdom's Strategy for Countering International Terrorism*, March 2009.

13 The Council of the European Union, *The European Union Counter-Terrorism Strategy*, 30 November 2005, p. 2.

Chapter Five

1   European Commission, 'On the identification and designation of European critical infrastructures and the assessment of the need to improve their protection', Council Directive 2008/114/EC, 8 December 2008, p. 3, available at http://eur-lex.europa.eu/LexUriServ/LexUriServ.do?uri=OJ:L:2008:345:0075:0082:EN:PDF.

2   See summaries on http://ec.europa.eu/home-affairs/funding/cips/funding_cips_en.htm.

Chapter Six

1   See Alistair Moffat, *Before Scotland: The Story of Scotland Before History* (London: Thames & Hudson, 2005), pp. 170, 177; Thorvaldur Thordarson and Stephen Self, 'Atmospheric and Environmental Effects of the 1783–1784 Laki Eruption: A Review and Reassessment', *Journal of Geophysical Research*, vol. 108, no. D1, 4011, doi: 10.1029.2001JD002042, 2003; Stephen Sparks et al., *Super-eruptions: Global Effects and Future Threats*, Report of a Geological Society of London Working Group, 2nd (print) ed., 2005, p. 11; Helgi Skuli Kjartansson, 'The Onset of Emigration from Iceland', *American Studies in Scandinavia*, vol. 10, no. 1, 1977, pp. 87–93.

2   For the concept of 'black swans' – high-impact, low-probability and hard-to-predict events – and their role in historical events see Nassim Nicholas Taleb, *The Black Swan: The Impact of the Highly Improbable* (London: Penguin, 2008).

3   *Topics 2000: Natural Catastrophes – the Current Position* (Munich: Munich Re, 2001).

4   This discussion of tectonic risks draws on a large number of disparate sources. Among the most important are data and publications of US Geological Survey Earthquakes Hazards Program, http://earthquake.usgs.gov/; the Italian National Institute of Geophysics and Vulcanology, http://portale.ingv.it/; and the Global Seismic Hazards Assessment Program, http://www.seismo.ethz.ch/GSHAP/.

5   Peter Sammonds et al., *Volcanic Hazard from Iceland: Analysis and Implications of the Eyjafjallajökull Eruption* (London: UCL Institute for Risk and Disaster Reduction, 2010), p. 1.

6   Thordarson and Self, (2003); Sparks et al., (2005), p. 11.

7   Helgi Skuli Kjartansson, 'The Onset of Emigration from Iceland', *American Studies in Scandinavia*, vol. 10, no. 1, 1977, pp. 87–93.

8   Emma Pryer, 'Volcano Expert Warns of Another Icelandic Eruption', *Daily Express*, 11 June 2010.

9   Dipartimento della Protezione Civile, Italy, *Pianificazione Nazionale D'Emergenza Dell'Area Vesuviana*, September 1995.

10 Paolo Gasparini, Franco Barberi and Attilio Belli, 'Early Warning of Volcanic Eruptions and Earthquakes in the Neapolitan area, Campania Region, South Italy', abstract from the Second International Conference

on Early Warning, Bonn, Germany, 16-18 October 2003, http://www.ewc2.org/upload/downloads/Gasparini2003AbstractEWC2.pdf.

11   Eurocontrol, 'Volcanic Ash Cloud Timeline – April Events', 12 May 2010, http://www.eurocontrol.int/corporate/public/standard_page/volcanic_ash_cloud_chronology.html; for the estimate of costs see EU Transport Commissioner Siim Kallas, quoted in 'EU Moves to Heal $3.3B Losses From Volcano', AP, 27 April 2010.

12   Sammonds et al., pp. 1–2.

13   Global Resources Information Database – Europe, *Impacts of Summer 2003 Heat Wave in Europe*, Environment Alert Bulletin 2 (Nairobi: United Nations Environment Programme, March 2004), http://www.grid.unep.ch/product/publication/download/ew_heat_wave.en.pdf. Calculation of both human and economic impacts are subject to various assumptions and uncertainties. For a discussion of some of these, see United Nations Environment Programme, *Global Environmental Outlook 3* (London: Earthscan, 2002), pp. 270–71.

14   'Russian Heatwave Caused 11,000 Deaths in Moscow: Official', AFP, 17 September 2010.

15   David Appell, 'Cost of Russia's Heat Wave', 5 August 2010, http://davidappell.blogspot.com/2010/08/cost-of-russias-heat-wave.html.

16   Jane Toothill, *Central European Flooding: August 2002*, EQECAT Technical Report, http://www.eqe.com/resources/Catastrophe_Reports/flood_rept.pdf.

17   Nick Britten, Nick Allen and Gary Cleland, 'Tidal Surge "Devastation" Averted by Minutes', *Daily Telegraph*, 9 November 2007. See also UK Environment Agency, *Review of 2007 Summer Floods* (Bristol: Environment Agency, 2007).

18   Jay Gulledge, 'Climate Risks: Lessons from 2010's Extreme Weather', Pew Centre on Global Climate Change, 23 August 2010, http://www.pewclimate.org/blog/gulledgej/climate-risks-lessons-from-2010%E2%80%99s-extreme-weather.

19   IPCC, *Climate Change 2007: The Physical Science Basis*, Working Group I Contribution to the Fourth Assessment Report (Cambridge: Cambridge University Press, 2007), Summary for Policymakers, pp. 5, 12–14.

20   See for example Katherine Richardson et al., *Synthesis Report from Climate Change: Global Risks, Challenges & Decisions, Copenhagen 2009, 10–12 March* (Copenhagen: University of Copenhagen, 2009); Pew Center for Global Climate Change, *Key Scientific Developments since the IPCC Fourth Assessment Report*, Science Brief 2, June 2009; various Final Reports of Synthesis and Assessment Products of the US Climate Change Science Program, available at http://www.gcrio.org/library/sap-final-reports.htm.

21   N.S. Keenlyside et al., 'Advancing Decadal-scale Climate Prediction in the North Atlantic Sector', *Nature*, 1 May 2008, pp. 84–9; Doug M. Smith et al., 'Improved Surface Temperature Prediction for the Coming Decade from a Global Climate Model', *Science*, 10 August 2007, pp. 796–99; for discussion of these technical studies, see Richard Wood, 'Natural Ups and Downs', *Nature Reports Climate Change*, vol. 2, May 2008, pp. 61–2.

22   *Attitudes of European Citizens Towards the Environment*, Special Eurobarometer 295, European Commission, March 2008.

23 Diarmid Campbell-Lendrum and Roberto Bertollini, 'Science, Media and Public Perception: Implications for Climate and Health Policies', *Bulletin of the World Health Organisation*, vol. 88, no. 4 (April 2010), p. 242.

24 See 'Climate Science: Well Done, Could Do Better', *IISS Strategic Comments*, vol. 16, no. 34 (October 2010).

25 Jonathan Leake, 'UN Wrongly Linked Global Warming to Natural Disasters', *Sunday Times*, 24 January 2010; 'IPCC Statement on Trends in Disaster Losses', 25 January 2010, http://www.ipcc.ch/pdf/presentations/statement_25_01_2010.pdf.

26 See IPCC, *Climate Change 2007: Impacts, Adaptation and Vulnerability*, Working Group II Contribution to the Fourth Assessment Report (Cambridge: Cambridge University Press, 2007), p. 547; Netherlands Environmental Assessment Agency, *Assessing an IPCC Assessment: An Analysis of Statements on Projected Regional Impacts in the 2007 Report* (The Hague: NEAA, 2010), pp. 89–95.

27 See Bastian Giegerich and Alexander Nicoll, eds, *European Military Capabilities: Building Armed Forces for Modern Operations*, IISS Strategic Dossier (London: IISS, 2008), ch. 3.

28 Council of the European Union, *Climate Change and International Security*, Report from the Commission and the Secretary-General/High Representative to the European Council, 7249/08, Brussels, 3 March 2008, available at http://register.consilium.europa.eu/pdf/en/08/st07/st07249.en08.pdf.

29 See for example European Commission, *Towards a Stronger European Disaster Response: The Role of Civil Protection and Humanitarian Assistance*, Communication from the Commission to the European Parliament and the Council, Com(2010) 600 final, 26 October 2010, available at http://ec.europa.eu/commission_2010-2014/georgieva/files/themes/european_disaster_response_capacity/final text EN.pdf.

30 See 'Pakistan's Floods: Broader Implications' *IISS Strategic Comments*, vol. 16, no. 29 (September 2010).

31 See Peter Stott, 'Climate Change: How to Play Our Hand', *Guardian*, 9 August 2010; Gulledge, 'Climate Risks: Lessons from 2010's Extreme Weather'.

32 Council of the European Union, *Climate Change and International Security*, Report from the Commission and the Secretary-General/High Representative to the European Council, 7249/08, Brussels, 3 March 2008.

Chapter Seven

1 European Union, 'A Secure Europe in a Better World – European Security Strategy', 12 December 2003, p.3, www.consilium.europa.eu/uedocs/cmsUpload/78367.pdf. 'Weapons of mass destruction' is an imprecise term that encompasses a variety of weapons and threats, ranging from relatively low-impact chemical weapons or radiological dispersal devices, to nuclear weapons that could destroy a large city. For the purpose

of this analysis, WMD proliferation is defined as the horizontal spread of nuclear, radiological, chemical and biological weapons, as well as their constituent materials, to states and non-state actors. It does not include missile or conventional-weapons proliferation, or broader issues relating to European nuclear postures or doctrines.

2   Council of the European Union, 'Thessaloniki European Council 19-20 June 2003 Presidency Conclusions', 11638/03, 1 October 2003, p.37. http://www.consilium.europa.eu/uedocs/cms_data/docs/pressdata/en/ec/76279.pdf.

3   Since its establishment, this role has been filled by Annalisa Giannella.

4   ESS, p.3.

5   Council of the European Union, 'EU strategy against proliferation of Weapons of Mass Destruction', 15708/03, 10 December 2003, pp.2-3, http://register.consilium.europa.eu/pdf/en/03/st15/st15708.en03.pdf.

6   Ibid., p.2.

7   Ibid., p.4.

8   See Council of the European Union, 'Council Conclusions and new lines for action by the European Union in combating the proliferation of weapons of mass destruction and their delivery systems', 17172/09, 17 December 2008.

9   European Union, 'Report on the Implementation of the European Security Strategy – Providing Security in a Changing World', S407/08, 11 December 2008, p.3.

10   WMD Strategy, p.8.

11   Ibid., p. 6.

12   For Joint Actions pertaining to BTWC see: Council Joint Action 2008/858/CFSP (10 November 2008), Council Joint Action 2006/184/CFSP (27 February 2006); for CTBTO see: Council Joint Action 2008/588/CFSP (15 July 2008), Council Joint Action 2007/468/CFSP (28 June 2007), Council Joint Action 2006/243/CFSP (20 March 2006); for IAEA see: Council Joint Action 2008/314/CFSP (14 April 2008), Council Joint Action 2007/753/CFSP (19 November 2007), Council Joint Action 2006/418/CFSP (12 June 2006), Council Joint Action 2005/574/CFSP (18 July 2005), Council Joint Action 2004/495/CFSP (17 May 2004); for OPCW see: Council Joint Action 2007/185/CFSP (19 March 2007), Council Joint Action 2005/913/CFSP (12 December 2005), Council Joint Action 2004/797/CFSP (22 November 2004); for WHO see: Council Joint Action 2008/307/CFSP (14 April 2008).

13   See Council of the European Union, 'Security-related export controls I - Dual use items and technology', http://www.consilium.europa.eu/showPage.aspx?id=408&lang=en.

14   See Nuclear black markets : Pakistan, A.Q. Khan and the rise of proliferation networks: a net assessment (London: International Institute for Strategic Studies, 2007).

15   See Council Joint Action 2008/368/CFSP (14 May 2008) and Council Joint Action 2006/419/CFSP of 12 June 2006.

16   'Communication from the Commission to the European Parliament and Council on Strengthening Chemical, Biological, Radiological and Nuclear Security in the European Union – an EU CBRN Action Plan', June 2009, http://ec.europa.eu/justice_home/news/summary/docs/com_2009_0273_en.pdf

17   See Council of the European Union, 'Non-Proliferation: Support of the Proliferation Security Initiative (PSI)', 10052/04, 1 June 2004, http://

www.consilium.europa.eu/uedocs/
cmsUpload/st10052.en04.pdf

[18] WMD Strategy, p.7.

[19] Javier Solana, 'European Proposals for Strengthening Disarmament and the Non-Proliferation Regime', PES Conference on 'Peace and Disarmament: A World Without Nuclear Weapons?', European Parliament, 9 December 2008, http://www.consilium.europa. eu/uedocs/cms_data/docs/pressdata/ en/discours/104602.pdf.

[20] In response to questioning in a European Parliament subcommittee in June 2010, the Personal Representative on Nonproliferation of WMD admitted that the differing nuclear status of EU states meant that 'tensions were there all the time' and that interests did not always converge. See 'Parliamentary Update (SEDE Subcommittee) 2 June 2010', ISIS Europe, http://www. isis-europe.org/pdf/2010_artrel_521_ epupdate-sede-02june10.pdf.

[21] In October 2010, France's President Nicolas Sarkozy reportedly told German Chancellor Angela Merkel and Russian President Dmitry Medvedev that 'France is not going to give up on its nuclear deterrent, whether or not this will disappoint you.' See 'Sarkozy: France to Hold Onto Nukes', Global Security Newswire, 20 October 2010, http://gsn.nti.org/gsn/ nw_20101020_1180.php.

[22] Speech by HR Catherine Ashton, at the Nuclear Non-Proliferation Treaty Review Conference, New York, 3 May 2010, http://www.consilium.europa. eu/uedocs/cms_data/docs/pressdata/ EN/foraff/114169.pdf.

[23] EU-US Summit, Washington, 2 November 2009, Council of the European Union, 15352/09, p.13, http://www.consilium.europa.eu/

uedocs/cms_data/docs/pressdata/en/ er/110929.pdf#page=13.

[24] See G8 Global Partnership, Council of the European Union, http://www. consilium.europa.eu/showPage. aspx?id=1226&lang=EN.

[25] 'Communication from the Commission to the European Parliament and Council on Strengthening Chemical, Biological, Radiological and Nuclear Security in the European Union – an EU CBRN Action Plan', June 2009, http://ec.europa.eu/ justice_home/news/summary/docs/ com_2009_0273_en.pdf.

[26] See 'Six-monthly Progress Report on the implementation of the EU Strategy against the proliferation of Weapons of Mass Destruction (2010/I)', 11135/10, 14 June 2010, register.consilium.europa. eu/pdf/en/10/st11/st11135.en10.pdf, p. 6.

[27] Ibid., p. 39.

[28] Communication with European threat reduction expert, August 2010. For more detail on planned regional centres of excellence on CBRN, see Commission of the European Communities, 'The Instrument for Stability – Multi-annual Indicative Programme 2009-2011', 8 April 2009, http://ec.europa.eu/ europeaid/how/finance/documents/ eidhr/ifs_ip_2009_2011_en.pdf.

[29] See 'EU statement in support of the Global Initiative to Combat Nuclear Terrorism (GICNT)', 17 June 2008, http://www.consilium.europa.eu/ uedocs/cms_Data/docs/pressdata/en/ misc/101246.pdf.

[30] 'Statement by President Herman Van Rompuy, on behalf of the European Union at the Nuclear Security Summit in Washington', 12 April 2010, http:// www.consilium.europa.eu/uedocs/ cms_Data/docs/pressdata/en/ ec/113709.pdf.

31 'Six-monthly Progress Report on the implementation of the EU Strategy against the proliferation of Weapons of Mass Destruction (2010/I)', 11135/10, 14 June 2010, register.consilium.europa.eu/pdf/en/10/st11/st11135.en10.pdf , p. 44.

32 'Preventing proliferation of WMD: the EU contribution', House of Lords, European Union Committee, 13ᵗʰ Report of Session 2004–5, 5 April 2005, p.21.

33 See Lina Grip, *The EU Non-Proliferation Clause: A Preliminary Assessment*, SIPRI Background Paper, November 2009, http://books.sipri.org/files/misc/SIPRIBP0911.pdf; and Gerrard Quille, 'The EU's Approach to Tackling The Proliferation of Materials and Weapons of Mass Destruction and Prospects for Cooperation on the Eve of a New US Administration', Working Paper, Directorate General External Policies of the Union, November 2008, http://www.europarl.europa.eu/meetdocs/2009_2014/documents/sede/dv/sede070909briefingpapernpt_/sede070909briefingpapernpt_en.pdf.

34 'New Lines', p.22.

35 Grip, *The EU Non-Proliferation Clause*, p.6.

36 The Council of the European Union has indeed published bi-annual reports on the implementation of the WMD Strategy. See 'Six-monthly Progress Report on the implementation of the EU Strategy against the proliferation of Weapons of Mass Destruction (2010/I)', 11135/10, 14 June 2010, register.consilium.europa.eu/pdf/en/10/st11/st11135.en10.pdf.

37 *EU Strategy against the proliferation of WMD: Monitoring and enhancing consistent implementation*, Council of the European Union, 16694/06, 12 December 2006.

38 *Preventing proliferation of WMD: the EU contribution*, (op cit).

39 'New Lines', p.4.

40 'New Lines', p.5.

41 Council of the European Union, 'Implementation of the WMD Strategy – Updated List of Priorities', 10747/08, 17 June 2008, p.12, http://register.consilium.europa.eu/pdf/en/08/st10/st10747.en08.pdf.

42 Oliver Meier, Interview with Annalisa Giannella, *Arms Control Today*, 16 February 2009, http://www.armscontrol.org/interviews/20090216_Giannella.

43 Much of the material from the following section is adapted from Ben Rhode, 'Nuclear proliferation: threats to European security from a nuclear Iran', in: B. Giegerich and V. Comolli eds., (2009), *FORESEC D4.5 Report on European Security, Trends Drivers, Threats*, 21 August 2009, pp.80-96, http://www.foresec.eu/wp3_docs/FORESEC_Deliverable_D_4_5.pdf.

44 UNSCR 1696 (August 2006); UNSCR 1737 (December 2006); UNSCR 1747 (March 2007); UNSCR 1803 (March 2008); UNSCR 1835 (September 2008), UNSCR 1929 (June 2010).

45 IAEA, *Implementation of the NPT Safeguards Agreement and relevant provisions of Security Council resolutions 1737 (2006), 1747 (2007), 1803 (2008) and 1835 (2008) in the Islamic Republic of Iran*, GOV/2009/35, 5 June 2009, p.4.

46 For a detailed examination of the proposed fuel-swap scheme, see Mark Fitzpatrick, 'Iran: the fragile promise of the fuel-swap plan', *Survival*, vol. 52 no. 3, June–July 2010, pp. 67–94.

47 Since 2009 evidence has emerged suggesting that Iran's research into nuclear weapons development continued after 2003, and may be

ongoing. In February 2010 the IAEA Director General reported that the information available to the Agency was 'extensive ... and broadly consistent and credible in terms of technical detail, the time frame ... and the people and organisations involved' and raised concerns about 'the possible existence in Iran of past or current undisclosed activities related to the development of a nuclear payload for a missile.' See IAEA, *Implementation of the NPT Safeguards Agreement and relevant provisions of Security Council resolutions 1737 (2006), 1747 (2007), 1803 (2008) and 1835 (2008) in the Islamic Republic of Iran*, GOV/2010/10, 3 March 2010, para 41.

48 Council of the European Union, *EU-Iran Basic Facts*, April 2009, http://www.consilium.europa.eu/uedocs/cmsUpload/EU-IRAN_Basic_facts_April_2009.pdf.

49 IAEA, *Implementation of the NPT Safeguards Agreement and relevant provisions of Security Council resolutions in the Islamic Republic of Iran*, GOV/2010/46, 6 September 2010.

50 James Blitz, Roula Khalaf and Daniel Dombey, 'Suggestions of Iran nuclear sabotage', *Financial Times*, 22 July 2010.

51 For a detailed evaluation of Iran's ballistic missile development, see *Iran's ballistic missile capabilities* (London: The International Institute for Strategic Studies, 2010).

52 In February 2010 the US Director of National Intelligence testified to Congress that Iran was 'technically capable of producing enough HEU for a weapon in the next few years, if it chooses to do so', and that Iran was 'keeping open the option to build nuclear weapons...should it chose to do so'. He added that 'we do not

know, however, if Iran will eventually decide to build nuclear weapons'. The previous year, he had testified that the US intelligence community assessed that Iran had not yet decided to produce HEU or to weaponise it for use as ballistic missile warhead. See Dennis C. Blair, *Annual Threat Assessment of the US Intelligence Community for the House Permanent Select Committee on Intelligence*, 3 February 2010, p.14; and Peter Finn, 'US, Israel Disagree on Iran Arms Threat', *Washington Post*, 11 March 2009.

53 For example, see Fareed Zakaria, 'They May Not Want the Bomb', *Newsweek*, 23 May 2009; Barry R. Posen, 'We Can Live With a Nuclear Iran', *The New York Times*, 27 February 2006; Christopher Hemmer, 'Responding to a Nuclear Iran', *Parameters*, http://www.carlisle.army.mil/usawc/parameters/07autumn/hemmer.pdf.

54 See Normon Podhoretz, 'Stopping Iran: Why the Case for Military Action Still Stands', *Commentary*, February 2008; Noah Feldman, 'Islam, Terror and the Second Nuclear Age', *New York Times Magazine*, 29 October 2006; Michael Rubin, 'Can a Nuclear Iran Be Contained or Deterred?', *AEI Online*, November 2008, http://www.aei.org/docLib/20081105_0823654MEO_g.pdf.

55 Speech by Catherine Ashton, at the League of Arab States, 'A Commitment to Peace – the European Union and the Middle East', 15 March 2010, http://www.consilium.europa.eu/uedocs/cms_data/docs/pressdata/EN/foraff/113352.pdf.

56 For an in-depth examination of this threat, see Fitzpatrick, ed., *Nuclear Programmes in the Middle East: In the shadow of Iran* (London: International Institute for Strategic Studies, 2008).

57 See *Nuclear Black Markets: Pakistan, A.Q. Khan and the rise of proliferation networks* (London: International Institute for Strategic Studies, 2007), p. 160.

58 See 'The EU and the Middle East Peace Process', EU External Action Service website, http://www.eeas.europa.eu/mepp/index_en.htm.

59 In 2010 leaked US military documents suggested that Iran had been providing extensive support to al-Qaeda and Taliban insurgents in Afghanistan. See Roula Khalaf, 'New light shed on claims Iran aided Taliban'; and Kenneth Katzman, *Iran: U.S. Concerns and Policy Responses*, p. 29

60 James Phillips, 'Hezbollah's Terrorist Threat to the European Union', *Heritage Lectures*, 28 August 2007.

61 *Intelligence and Security Committee Annual Report 2005–6*, p.5, http://www.cabinetoffice.gov.uk/media/cabinetoffice/corp/assets/publications/reports/intelligence/annualiro506.pdf

62 'Iran in 'backroom offers' to West', *BBC News*, 20 February 2009, http://news.bbc.co.uk/1/hi/world/europe/7901101.stm.

63 For further detail, see Tom Sauer, 'Struggling on the World Scene: An Over-ambitious EU versus a Committed Iran', *European Security*, vol. 17, nos. 2–3, June–September 2008; Fitzpatrick, *The Iranian Nuclear Crisis*, pp. 23–26 and Gary Samore ed.; *Iran's Strategic Weapons Programmes: A Net Assessment* (London: Routledge, 2005), pp. 15–31.

64 Examples include reports that Germany was prepared to tolerate limited enrichment within Iran, or that certain non-E3 states were dissatisfied with what they perceived to be an inflexible diplomatic approach. European countries including Greece, Cyprus, Spain, Malta, Italy, Austria, Sweden and Denmark have expressed their reluctance or opposition to imposing stricter sanctions against Iran. See Sauer, 'Struggling on the World Scene', and Elisa Oezbek, 'The EU's Nonproliferation Strategy: Iran as a Test Case', *Strategic Assessment*, vol. 13, no. 2, August 2010, p. 73.

65 George Jahn, 'Iran Defiant in Nuclear Documents', *Associated Press*, 6 August 2010.

66 Reports in 2010 suggested that official statistics ignored Iran-China trade channelled via the UAE which, if taken into account, would mean China had surpassed the EU to become Iran's largest trading partner. See Najmeh Bozorgmehr and Geoff Dyer, 'China Overtakes EU as Iran's Top Trade Partner', *Financial Times*, 8 February 2010.

67 Benjamin Weinthal, 'Iran Sanctions: The German Control Problem', *PolicyWatch* 1543, Washington Institute for Near East Policy, 26 June 2009; Emanuele Ottolenghi, *Under a Mushroom Cloud: Europe, Iran and the Bomb* (London: Profile Books, 2009), pp.152–198; European Commission, 'Bilateral Trade Relations – Iran', http://trade.ec.europa.eu/doclib/docs/2006/september/tradoc_113392.pdf; 'Foreign Trade - Ranking of Germany's trading partners in foreign trade, 2008', *Statistisches Bundesamt*, 3 March 2009, http://www.destatis.de/jetspeed/portal/cms/Sites/destatis/Internet/EN/Content/Statistics/Aussenhandel/Handelspartner/Tabellen/Content100/RangfolgeHandelspartner,property=file.pdf.

68 Fitzpatrick, *The Iranian Nuclear Crisis*, pp. 37–39; Katzman, *Iran: U.S. Concerns and Policy Responses*, p. 47.

[69] See *Six-monthly Progress Report on the implementation of the EU Strategy against the proliferation of Weapons of Mass Destruction (2010/I)*, p. 17

[70] See Leigh Phillips, 'EU Iran sanctions "most far-reaching ever agreed"', EUobserver, 23 July 2010, http://euobserver.com/24/30534.

[71] By October 2010 there were indications that the Iranian regime was encountering severe economic problems, some of which were caused or exacerbated by international sanctions. See Thomas Erdbink, 'Sanctions Begin to Compound Iran's Severe Economic Problems', *Washington Post*, 5 October 2010.

Chapter Eight

[1] A. Checchi, A. Behrens and C. Egenhofer, 'Long-term energy security risks for Europe: A sector-specific approach', CEPS Working Document 309, January 2009, pp. 1–3.

[2] *Ibid.*, p. 2; See also A. Dupont, 'The strategic implications of climate change', *Survival* vol. 50, no. 3), June–July 2008, pp. 34–35.

[3] European Commission, 'Securing your energy future: Commission presents energy security, solidarity and efficiency proposals', *Press Release IP/08/1696*, 13 November 2008.

[4] N. Elhefnawy, 'The Impending Oil Shock', *Survival* vol. 50, no. 2, April–May 2008, p.37.

[5] Checchi et al., p.3.

[6] BP, *BP Statistical Review of World Energy 2010*, June 2010, p. 2.

[7] *Ibid.*, p. 7.

[8] BP, *BP Statistical Review of World Energy*, (2007).

[9] Elhefnawy, p.38.

[10] See, for example, Muyin Wang and James E. Overland, 'A sea-ice free summer Arctic within 30 years?', *Geophysical Research Letters*, vol. 36, L. 07502, 2009, available at http://mrc.org/pdf/WANG-OVERLAND-ARCTIC%20SEA%20ICE%20ESTIMATE.pdf.

[11] A.E. Kramer, 'Russia-Ukraine Feud Goes Beyond Gas Pipes', *The New York Times*, (4 January 2009).

[12] Anatoly Medetsky,'Deal Struck on Gas, Black Sea Fleet', *The Moscow Times*, 22 April 2010.

[13] Tim Webb, 'Belarus Energy Supplies', *The Guardian*, 3 January 2010.

[14] A.B. Kushner, 'Not a Safe Route', *Newsweek*, 23 August 2008.

[15] I. Talley, 'US Envoy: Next Step for Nabucco Is Facilitating Gas Supply', *The Wall Street Journal*, 20 July 2009.

[16] BBC, 'Saudi Arabia Detains Dozens of 'al-Qaeda Militants'', 24 March 2010.

[17] P.W. Parfomak, 'Pipeline Security: An Overview of Federal Activities and Current Policy Issues', *CRS Report for Congress*, 5 February 2004, pp. 4–6.

[18] Swiss Federal Office of Energy, *Report on the blackout in Italy on 28 September 2003*, pp. 5–6.

[19] Eurostat calculates import dependency using the following formula: Import Dependency = Net Imports / (Bunkers+Gross Inland Consumption). Negative numbers indicate that the country is a net exporter. Values over 100% are possible due to changes in stocks.

[20] Map adapted from: *Strategic Survey 2008* (London: Routledge for IISS, 2008).

[21] Mark Leonard and Nicu Popescu, 'A Power Audit of EU-Russia relations', *ECFR report*, 7 November 2007, pp. 25–50.

[22] Paul Belkin, 'The European Union's Energy Security Challenges', *CRS Report for Congress*, 2008, pp. 15–17.

[23] *Ibid.*, p. 18.

[24] At the time of writing the Medgaz pipeline to Spain is expected to be operational in July 2010 after several postponements. The GALSI pipeline to Italy is expected to be operational in 2012.

[25] David Buchan, *Energy and Climate Change: Europe and the Crossroads* (Oxford: Oxford University Press, 2009), p. 86.

[26] See http://epp.eurostat.ec.europa.eu/portal/page/portal/eurostat/home/. Definitions: % Total Consumption = Crude Oil/Petroleum Products Gross Inland Consumption (TJNCV)/All Products Gross Inland Consumption (TJNCV). Import Dependency = Net Imports (TJNCV)/Bunkers + Gross Inland Consumption (TJNCV). % Import Supply = Russia or OPEC Imports (1000T)/Total Imports(1000T)

[27] In the case of Natural Gas, % Import Supply was calculated using imports in TJGCV.

[28] European Commission, 'Europe's Current and future energy position. Demand – resources – investments', *An EU Energy Security and Solidarity Action Plan*, 2008, pp. 9–10.

[29] Checchi et al., pp. 27–28.

[30] European Nuclear Society, 'Nuclear Power Plants in Europe', 1 October 2010 http://www.euronuclear.org/info/encyclopedia/n/nuclear-power-plant-europe.htm.

[31] International Energy Agency, 2005, in *ibid.*, pp. 27–28.

[32] Frank Barnaby, *The nuclear renaissance: Nuclear weapons proliferation and terrorism* (London: Institute for Public Policy Research, March 2009).

[33] IAEA, *Fast Reactor Database 2006 Update*, http://www-frdb.iaea.org/auxiliary/generalInformation.html.

[34] World Nuclear Association, *Advanced Nuclear Power Reactors*, updated 14 October 2010 http://www.world-nuclear.org/info/default.aspx?id=528&terms=FBR.

[35] BBC, 'Germany Agrees to Extend Nuclear Plant Life Span', 6 September 2010.

[36] Checchi et al., p. 25.

[37] European Commission, 'EU adopts new rules strengthening the internal energy market', Press Release IP/09/1038, (25 June 2009).

[38] Buchan, *Energy and Climate Change: Europe and the Crossroads*, p. 81.

[39] Dupont, 'The strategic implications of climate change', p. 34.

[40] Belkin, 'The European Union's Energy Security Challenges', p. 10.

[41] The Treaty, together with the Energy Charter Protocol on Energy Efficiency and Related Environmental Aspects, was signed in 1994. It is a legally-binding instrument signed by 51 states, the EC and Euratom http://www.encharter.org/index.php?id=7&L=0 President Putin rejected the Treaty in 2009.

[42] *Ibid.*, p. 17.

[43] A. Myers Jaffe and R. Soligo, 'Re-evaluating US strategic priorities in the Caspian Region: balancing energy resource initiatives with terrorism containment', *Cambridge Review of International Affairs* vol. 17, no. 2, July 2004, p. 262.

44 For information on world energy reserves and supplies, see BP Statistical Review of World Energy June 2010.

45 Ruslan Krivobok, 'Russia, Ukraine to Consider Joint Atomic Project', *Rianovosti*, 19 July 2010.

Concluding Remarks

1 Speech by President of the European Commission José Manuel Durão Barroso, European Union, Strasbourg 7 September, SPEECH/10/441, p. 7.

2 This problematique has long been captured by the term 'capablities–expectations gap', coined by political scientist Christopher Hill, 'The Capabilities–Expectations Gap, or Conceptualising Europe's International Role', Journal of Common Market Studies, vol. 31, no. 3, 1993, pp. 305–28.

3 Sven Biscop and Jo Coelmont, 'A Strategy for CSDP: Europe's Ambitions as a Global Security Provider', Egmont Paper no. 37 (Brussels: Egmont Institute, 2010).

Adelphi books are published eight times a year by Routledge Journals, an imprint of Taylor & Francis, 4 Park Square, Milton Park, Abingdon, Oxfordshire OX14 4RN, UK.

A subscription to the institution print edition, ISSN 0567-932X, includes free access for any number of concurrent users across a local area network to the online edition, ISSN 1478-5145.

2010 Annual Adelphi Subscription Rates			
Institution	£457	$803 USD	€673
Individual	£230	$391 USD	€312
Online only	£433	$763 USD	€640

Dollar rates apply to subscribers outside Europe. Euro rates apply to all subscribers in Europe except the UK and the Republic of Ireland where the pound sterling price applies. All subscriptions are payable in advance and all rates include postage. Journals are sent by air to the USA, Canada, Mexico, India, Japan and Australasia. Subscriptions are entered on an annual basis, i.e. January to December. Payment may be made by sterling cheque, dollar cheque, international money order, National Giro, or credit card (Amex, Visa, Mastercard).

For more information, visit our website: **http://www.informaworld.com/ adelphipapers.**

For a complete and up-to-date guide to Taylor & Francis journals and books publishing programmes, and details of advertising in our journals, visit our website: **http://www.informaworld.com.**

Ordering information:
USA/Canada: Taylor & Francis Inc., Journals Department, 325 Chestnut Street, 8th Floor, Philadelphia, PA 19106, USA. **UK/Europe/Rest of World:** Routledge Journals, T&F Customer Services, T&F Informa UK Ltd., Sheepen Place, Colchester, Essex, CO3 3LP, UK.

Advertising enquiries to:
USA/Canada: The Advertising Manager, Taylor & Francis Inc., 325 Chestnut Street, 8th Floor, Philadelphia, PA 19106, USA. Tel: +1 (800) 354 1420. Fax: +1 (215) 625 2940.

UK/Europe/Rest of World: The Advertising Manager, Routledge Journals, Taylor & Francis, 4 Park Square, Milton Park, Abingdon, Oxfordshire OX14 4RN, UK. Tel: +44 (0) 20 7017 6000. Fax: +44 (0) 20 7017 6336.

The print edition of this journal is printed on ANSI conforming acid-free paper by Bell & Bain, Glasgow, UK.

1944-5571(2010)50:4-5;1-E